ESOTERIC ESPLANADE.

Philip Fletcher

Copyright 2008-11-18

ISBN   978-0`9556879-4-5

For B and C who've always been kind to me.

ESOTERIC ESPLANADE.

(The beach road going nowhere in particular, except perhaps to the farthest reaches of the

endless night zone.)

This seventh and final collection is dedicated to Kayley, our one in a million Saturday girl, (the other 999,999 didn't want the job, ha, ha, ha!)

Yes folks, I'm finally embarking on putting my final most recent collection on to disc; I know at the end of my last collection: THE MEANING OF LIFE etc, I said I was finished with writing forever…Well forever didn't last very long, I think I slept through most of it. But this is definitely it, life's too short to keep churning out 'product' that no-one's reading, and I've got my old age to prepare for; if I make it that far down the long, lonely road that my life's been all about. I wanted to add something else equally witty, but it's slipped my mind, so fuck it! 20/9/04. Ah, I've remembered now, five days later, yes, these are the last of my parables for the lost and the lonely, they're on their own after this; maybe then I can have an end to irritable bowel syndrome and all the other anxiety-related health problems I suffer from.

....

5
I REFUSE.

I refuse to snooze through any more editions of 'POETRY PLEASE', I won't bother listening to it instead, when I'm lying in bed for want of nothing better to do. I refuse to please anyone other than myself. I refuse to pay £1 a minute (plus v.a.t., plus it's gone up to £1.50p now I think) to phone a likely candidate in METRO's 'lonely hearts' column; and even more strongly refuse, if I was able to afford it, to foot the bill for an evening out with a potential partner out of one of these columns if, indeed such a date could be made thru' the labyrinth of female psychology in these matters. And knowing from bitter experience how severely judgemental women can be when it comes to selecting a mate, I refuse not to hate judgemental women. I refuse to accuse myself of mysogyny. Mi/ysogyny? Who? Me!? I don't even know how to spell it properly. I refuse to carry on with this exercise any further, even tho' my public, (pause for appreciative murmurs of laughter) is begging me too.

....

A SOFT GREY LIGHT.

It's the dead of night and there's a soft, undefined grey light visible through my uncurtained bedroom window. The window's uncurtained because there's no need for privacy, there's no glass, there's nothing out there anymore.
This is my eternity, seemingly to be spent as I lived my life, alone. Hell isn't so much other people, rather than an absence of real and meaningful people in your life, when you had it.

....

A BAD DREAM IN A BAD REALITY.

I came choking and spluttering out of a bad dream, it was 4 am in my warm but lifeless hotel room in Brauneberg, West Germany. I had 3 hours to wait before I could go down for breakfast at 7 am, and another 90 minutes after that before I could commence the long journey home by coach.

As I lay there getting my head back together, I said out loud in a dead-pan voice, 'It's just a bad dream,' and then about 30 seconds later, 'in a bad reality'. It was a little later when I thought, 'A bad dream in a bad reality sums up my life now, there's virtually no escape from the awful impasse I'm in, unless I could afford to go and live in a certain part of Thailand, and either get married or have a string of lovers.'

I'd forgotten to bring my travel alarm clock, which, unless I'd stuck it in the wardrobe under some clothes, would have kept me awake all night with its monotonous ticking. I would have been awakened by its high-pitched alarm even if I'd had a lead lined safe to put it in. I wanted to be down for breakfast at 7 am to beat the rush, and also because I thought it would be quiet. I kept myself awake with some difficulty, checking my watch at regular intervals; I'd left the light on to help me stay awake, I narrowly avoided dozing off just before seven o'clock.

Imagine my chagrin after descending the four flights of stairs to reach the dining room, to be met with a barrage of wittering and twittering, a load of old fogies had beat me to it; I was in a black mood. Having helped myself to whatever I thought was edible in the dim electric light, I strode, shoulders hunched, looking straight ahead, to the back table; thankfully a big pot of coffee was standing on it. I'd no sooner sat down when even more of these chirping early birds came and clogged-up the seats round the table.

Almost as big a crime against my sensitive nature as their constant wittering, was the stink of perfume off some of the more gross females; I bolted my food and drink and exited the same way I'd entered, back to my room to kill the last 60 minutes of waiting time.

I'd gone to Germany for New Year in an attempt to escape being here on my own; the same reason I'd gone to Paris for Christmas, next year I'm going to try Blackpool. In fairness, both holidays had potential for enjoyment if you were 'up for it'. For instance, there was an optional night out in Paris on Christmas Eve, whose theme was eating, drinking, and singing; 27 euros, about £19. But I've become so introverted that the thought of drunkenly singing, 'Rudolph The Red-Nosed Reindeer' with a bunch of strangers, filled me with fear and dread. I decided to go to bed early instead and work up an appetite for 'Crimbo' dinner on the River Seine…and what a pile of French crap that turned out to be, not even any crimbo pud and custard to round the dismal repast off with. It was all downhill after that, I got drunk on the coach on the way back to Halifax to relieve the monotony of a long bum-numbing coach journey.

New Year's Eve in Brauneberg got off to a noisy start, the evening meal began at 7.30 pm and the festivities went on until the early hours. Not that I hung around to welcome the new year in, I'd had enough of party poppers and those horrible things that make a sound like a duck being strangled slowly when you blow into them, as well as picking streamers out of my food, before 10pm, and slunk off to my room to be alone, without even saying goodnight to the people I was sat at dinner with; I just wasn't 'up for it'. If I'd had a 'significant other' as Del-boy Trotter is fond of calling his long-suffering partner Raquel, I might have fared better; as it was I stuck out like the proverbial sore thumb, and my cheap intellectual snobbery meant I could no longer hardly be bothered to make the effort to be sociable; I detested most of the people I was with, a bad reality or what?

....

BONDING WITH NATURE.
(Blessed are those who don't give a damn.)

It was a lovely autumn morning last Friday, and even though I hadn't planned to go out, I felt compelled to take advantage of the soft breeze and bright sunshine. From my kitchen window I have a heart-warming view of the hills midway between Cornholme and Todmorden town centre. My enjoyment of this stunning view is marred by the houses in the immediate vicinity, especially the one opposite my bungalow's kitchen window; a rundown two storey council house, whose occupants I strongly suspect of constantly spying on me from their back bedroom window; so my appreciation of the hills is rather furtive.
Last Thursday lunchtime, after I'd done a two hour stint of word processing at Ashenhurst Community Centre, which is on Dinely Avenue, the last row of houses below the hills and farmland, I spotted the entrance to an access route into the countryside; I never knew it was there before then (the well worn path that is). I walked as far as a fork in the farm vehicle track, leading to a farmhouse on the right and an unknown destination on my left, I decided to return at some suitable point in the future to check the left fork out, that occasion being as soon as last Friday noon.
The soft breeze became a strong, cold wind by the time I'd climbed up to Dinely Avenue via the stepped, steep walkways, but I wasn't put off; I had my trusty woolly hat on, (now lost alas after 16 faithful years of service, Doh!), a lightweight 'windjammer' jacket, my thermal leggings and walking boots, all for a country stroll. I felt really impressed at finding this rural beauty spot

virtually on my doorstep, normally it's a bit of a trek to get away from the horrors of modern life, not least of which being people who I have nothing in common with, and who I dread having any contact with.

I reached the fork in the track and took the left turn, by which time I was in the mood to stay out as long as possible for as far as the path would take me. Imagine my disappointment when after about half a mile into the walk, I came up against another farmhouse blocking my way; the vehicle track stopped at its entrance. There was no gate barring access and no barking dogs, so I gingerly moved onto the property to see if I could rejoin the path on the other side of it. There was some very crunchy gravel at the side of this modernised dwelling, and a 4-wheel-drive vehicle neatly parked up; I felt very self-conscious doing my 'reccy', expecting to be challenged at any moment. Whoever lives there has chosen it for its perfectly secluded location; they might have been in seclusion while I was snooping about, because there was no sign of life. I couldn't make out any continuation of my route beyond this point, it was pastureland dropping down to my left, and steeply sloping hills to my right; I reluctantly turned back.

Normally, I'm not very brave or adventurous, I stick to the beaten path, so it came as a surprise to me shortly after I'd turned back, to decide to climb up one of the more accessible slopes to see what lay over its brow; no mean feat when you're 56, partially sighted, and not in peak condition. Luckily I found a sturdy piece of broken branch not far into my ascent, I literally had to go up grabbing tufts of long grass in front of me and digging the toes of my boots in, I didn't let fears of how was I going to get back down again put me off. A couple of times I stopped to get some breath back into my tortured lungs, and to see if the brow looked any nearer. It didn't, but neither did I feel a sense of panic that I'd made one of my frequent errors of judgement.

The sun was still shining brightly when I reached the top, feeling fairly certain I was going to collapse at any moment from this unaccustomed strenuous exercise. My heart was pounding, my legs were shaking, and too much blood had gone to my brain. After I'd recovered my breath I looked over the near fatally fought for vista, at some startled sheep to my left and a lovely wooded hill to my right, but no sign of any human inroads except inexplicably, an ancient length of dry-stone wall; what the hell was it doing up there!? I wasn't feeling intrepid enough to do any more exploring of the unknown terrain in front of me, I'd have needed to be much more agile and clued-up about orienteering for that.

Between where I was and Burnley could have been eight miles or so, only if I'd found a packhorse trail would I have continued walking; or if I'd been with an experienced walker. My boots came into their own in helping me to get back down again, along with the seat of my pants and my sturdy stick, but hey, I'm glad I did it!!!

It's occurred to me since, somewhat morbidly perhaps, that if I'd died from over exertion on the brow of that hill, it wouldn't have bothered me; for however long it would have taken to locate my mortal remains, and being coldly realistic, that could have been quite some time, weeks or even months if no one had spotted me heading off in that direction when I left home, my body would have been at one with the elements, and unless my specs were knocked off, no passing crow would have pecked my eyes out for a couple of small juicy morsels. It's hardly likely that I'd lie up there for 5,000 years like the skeletal remains of that ancient warrior they found in the Swiss Alps a few years ago, but maybe long enough for the worried and harassed look to leave my face and a look of peaceful repose replace it. I'd rather be dead out there than rotting and stinking in my bungalow.

(I never did go back out to that spot, there was such an iffy atmosphere on that little estate that quite frankly, I felt too afraid; I had visions of being buggered and murdered out there, a far cry from the stylised idealism of a noble end in splendid isolation. I was eventually harassed off the estate, thank fuck, and now I'm facing harassment of a different nature where I'm living, as highlighted in the very last entry in this, my very last collection. [Bar one, I don't know if it will be confusing to potential readers, me sticking these little asides in? But 'LONELIER THAN DEATH' has turned out to be my last collection. 4/7/06.] 24/9/04.)

....

I'm reproducing here a letter I wrote to David Blunkett MP, OUR CURRENT home Secretary, written and sent towards the end of last year, in order to flesh out the letter, I think I should quote the newspaper article that prompted it; I must say I'm astonished by Blunkett's moral hypocrisy regarding his affair with a married woman, that's come to light this year...

KILLER NILSEN LOSES FIGHT TO TELL STORY. by Gary Jones. Daily Mirror, Sat, 20/12/03.

'Gay serial killer Dennis Nilsen yesterday lost a High Court bid for the right to tell his macabre story. Nilsen was jailed in 1983 for the murders of at least six men. In a 400-page draft autobiography called Nilsen: History Of A Drowning Man, he tells how he abused, cut up and flushed his young victims body parts down the toilet at his home in North London.
Nilsen, 57, claimed he was being denied the right to 'freedom of expression' after the Governor of Full Sutton prison near York, where he's held, seized the manuscript. But Mr Justice Maurice Kay threw out Nilsen's request for a

Judicial Review of the governor's decision to refuse him access to the draft. He said his victims' families had the right not to read explicit details of a man whose crimes 'were as grave and depraved as it is possible to imagine'. Nilsen---caught after a plumber found body parts—is thought to have killed up to 15 men. He will never be released. Prison staff encouraged him to tell his story, believing it may help him understand why he carried out his crimes'.

....

Dear Mr. David Blunkett. MP,

I'm enclosing a clipping from Saturday's DAILY MIRROR (20/12/03) to illustrate my point. I don't condone for one minute what this man did, but it's grimly ironic that if he'd been writing those awful events purely from imagination, like the writer of the truly evil and perverted ' THE SILENCE OF THE LAMBS' saga for instance, it would have been permissible and highly popular. Shouldn't Nilsen's autobiography be at least made available to criminal psychologists and criminal profilers? Because more and more human 'time bombs' are suffering from social exclusion and isolation? I use writing letters as a means of communication.
We've never had real 'freedom of expression' in Britain, vested interests and the libel laws have seen to that; but I now feel we're entering into our most sinister phase of curbing 'free speech' ever; and you and your government are the architects of its destruction. 'new Labour' was elected to govern the country, not to try and control how we think and feel, like in George Orwell's 1984. If my memory serves me well, you wanted some legislation to curtail free speech even in the privacy of your own home? This seems like the mark of a true zealot; it's not so long ago that homosexual practices were only acceptable by consenting adults in the privacy of their own home.
With the insidious introduction of 'political correctness', more and more people have become 'thin skinned' and are ready to take offence at the slightest jibe. Well, Mr. Blunkett, I'm partially sighted, and when I was a kid, (that could be offensive to baby goats) (I'm nearly 57 now) my specs were like the proverbial 'jam jar bottoms', and yes, I grew up in the school of hard knocks and have been emotionally scarred as a result. But at the same time, I learned to defend myself, verbally if not physically; because everyone's got an aspect of themselves they don't like and don't want attention drawing to. If I'd been totally 'mollycoddled' as a child, how would I be able to deal with life's adversities? The number of which I've suffered you couldn't begin to imagine; you're one of the few disabled people who made it through a prejudiced society, and don't tell me it's easier for disabled people to find

suitable employment now, because it isn't. If you think it is, could you please find me a job in communications, your PA perhaps?

The government of the day was quick to come to the defence of Salman Rushdie after he published 'THE SATANIC VERSES', a book that I read and couldn't see what all the fuss and bloodshed was about; another example of Islamic fascism. And now we've got millions of them over here just biding their time until they become the 'first' religious faith in this country; I detest religion by the way, except Buddhism which is 99.9% pacifist.

My point is that nowadays, more and more publishers are afraid of publishing anything controversial for fear of offending vociferous minorities, and upsetting the imposed atmosphere of blandness being championed by New Labour; freedom of thought is being driven underground, let alone freedom of expression. Resulting in a paranoid schizophrenic atmosphere everywhere. Well Mr B, just like the 'proles' in 1984, I've got nothing to lose, because I'VE GOT NOTHING! I was born and bred in England and all I've ever heard is the sound of doors slamming shut in my face; all I've got left is my FREEDOM! Yours sincerely Mr Phil Fletcher.

(He never replied, and I dare say I'm on some government list of potential subversives. Only this week the BBC pulled a cartoon sereies scheduled for BBC3, called 'POPETOWN' because it might be deemed offensive to practicing Roman Catholics!!!! After it's been proven what a bunch of moral hypocrites that church has hosted, and that's putting it mildly PLF. 25/9/04.)

....

POSTERITY MY ARSE!

My life has mirrored that of Vincent Van Gogh to an alarming degree, loneliness, rejection, and isolation beyond compare in the modern world, (mind you, I've just heard of someone who's still a virgin at 38, the damn thing will have healed or shrivelled up by now, get rid darling before it's finally too late); I've also lived 20 years longer than he did, and on a good day I look forward to another 30 years or more.

In my arrogance I've assumed that one day, some time after I'm dead, my pathetic scrawlings will be 'discovered' by an opportunistic publisher who knows that the world loves a good sob story; we all love to read about sad bastards suffering, it makes us feel better. Hey! what am I saying? I'm the ultuimate sad bastard me, (apart from that 38-year-old virgin.) But unlike Vincent, I don't have a 'champion' in the shape of a magnanimous brother to support me; State Benefits are my life support system, I'd be a dead man for sure by now without them, from physical and mental exhaustion and, hopefully, alcoholism. But no, full blown alcoholism's one of the worst diseases to have, I should know, I've survived it.

To avoid being used and abused, like the memory of Vincent Van Gogh has been, (he hated the exploitative art market and its dealers, regarding them as no better than money lenders in the temple; but now his Impressionist paintings sell for astronomical prices, benefiting no-one but private individuals or corporations.) I've made my will out to WSPA, THE world Society for the Protection of Animals, incorporating copyright of all my writings, so that when my true worth is discovered, and even my most casual jottings (hand written of course), fetch a shed-load of cash, only the planet's sorely pressed eco systems will benefit, and not some bloated human parasite. But lately a nagging doubt's been crossing my mind, 'What if I never get discovered and my work dies with me'? All hopefully, neatly transferred onto floppy disc, (apart from my diaries and other sundries), which is already being supplanted by CD-writer and 'memory stick', whatever they are; according to Kayley, to whom this collection is dedicated. (She's only 18 you know, slurp, slurp!), I'd call it bitter posthumous irony, wouldn't you? Quite possibly, for every writer who makes it, a thousand don't; I've never heard of most of todays successful ones, and I'm not interested either. There's far too much 'product' on the market and I only read now because it's a cheap form of entertainment and passing the time, along with listening to music and watching television. Look what's happened to J.K. Rowling, she's now well on her way to becoming as obscenely rich as Paul McCartney, I'd only have respect for either of them if they gave most of their undeserved wealth away, to causes that would help to save some of the endangered species we've got so many of nowadays. My respect goes out to those who can write good scripts for TV and Radio, you can shove highbrow literature as far up your front or back bottoms as you can! I hate cold, over-intellectualised writing as much as I detest the modern art movement.

There's lots of paranoid, so-called moral censorship around these days, freedom of speech is under attack from the Home Office down, ask Robert Kilroy Silk, the longstanding reality TV daytime presenter who, until very recently, hosted a live discussion programme; but a controversial article he wrote about Arabs in a Sunday newspaper, has left his career in limbo; Muslims and the racial equality board are after his blood. I've written to the BBC in his defence, pointing out that they screened a programme the other week (TIMEWATCH I think) about the white slave trade of the 17th and 18th centuries, where an estimated 1.25 million white Europeans were kidnapped by Barbary Coast pirates and sold off as slaves in Morocco and Algeria. I knew nothing about this, all we hear about is the black slave trade and the evils of colonialism; how many of them were taken out of Africa? They always manage to colonise wherever they get a foothold, and make their former masters squirm with guilt. I'll be accused of writing hate literature when I say I wish neither blacks nor Muslims were here in Britain; so go on, arrest me, try me and 'disappear' me forever...again!

('Kilroy' has re-emerged as a key player in the UKIP movement, indeed he's now a Euro MP, along with 12 others; I voted UKIP this year.) (But since writing this piece I've seen Mr Kilroy Silk for what he really is, and he should have joined the Monster Raving Loony Party instead of founding his one-man party called 'VERITAS' or was it 'SHUVITUPYERASS'?)

....

Dear TODMORDEN NEWS,

what I find really galling about the fiend, Harold Shipman's death, is that he was apparently allowed the privilege of choosing when to take his own life! He wasn't on suicide watch and he was back on full privileges in Wakefield Prison.

Why was Britain's most notorious mass murderer allowed 'privileges' in the first place? He was there to be punished for his crimes against humanity. If I'd been prison governor he'd have been in a spartanly attired cell with photos of all his victims on the walls, and absolutely no contact with the outside world, especially his wife. He would have stayed in that condition until his natural death, and he would have been monitored for suicide attempts.

But no, cynically, Shipman has had the last laugh, he's beaten the rap; choosing to top himself (allegedly) just in time for his wife to receive a 'golden handshake' from the state in the form of a lump sum of £100,000, and £10,000 a year for as long as she lives; Shipman's pension entitlement; I'd block that too if I could, if a law's bad then change it...pronto!

Who says that crime doesn't pay, certainly not Primrose Shipman presumably? If that last remark is libellous I'd feel it a privilege to go to court to defend myself against her, because I'm a pauper relatively speaking; it would be like her trying to get blood out of a stone.

PS, I wonder what privileges Rose West is enjoying these days? Maybe she's allowed out on day release to run a crèche unsupervised, or perhaps she's allowed a weekly visit from an 'escort' who's deeply into S&M and bondage? (An edited version of this letter was published at the start of 2004. PLF.)

....

I'm assuming that the famous Phil (spectre) Speckter? spells his name thus, I've no way of verifying this though; I've thought of using Phil Spectre as a nom de plume but I can't find this word (which one?) in any of my 3 dictionaries, along with sobriquet, so I can't confirm what they mean. I seem

to live my life like a ghost, my existence matters only to me, and I haunt the real world, which taunts and mocks me with glimpses and tasters of what real life should be lived like; British women are totally evil CUNTS!
(I don't know why I couldn't find 'spectre' before, I've found it now and it confirms what I am; I was spelling sobriquet as 'subriquet' so that explains why I couldn't find that, and as for Phil Speckter? Because he's been in the news for allegedly murdering a woman, (I wonder why?), I've discovered his surname is spelt 'Spector'. So I could call myself Phil Spectre if I wanted to, which is how I always thought the famous '60s record producer's surname was spelt, because he's got such a creepy reputation; mystery solved.
CIVIL LIBERTY TAKERS.

Walking through my litter-strewn estate, hating the dumb scum who left this anti social statement on the pavement, grass verges, and privet hedges.
This human dirt probably thinks it is worth more than what it gets out of life, never mind the fact that as a parasitic germ it contributes nothing but negativity to society. Why can I never be free of this soul-destroying filth? This peculiarly English disease of envy and hate? It's getting almost too late for it to matter whether I escape or not, the subversive plot sickens and confounds me; WHY are these creatures so NAFF!? It's just as easy to do the right thing, and have a LAFF!

(Both the above pieces were written in the bleak mid-winter of 2 years ago, 2003.)

....

FORGOTTEN PLACES.

Like the old lanes too narrow for the detested car to get down, lined on either side with beautifully dressed stone walls over six feet tall with curved top-stones; what compelled these long dead people to put up these magnificent structures in such out of the way places? To invest such time and effort and cost!
There's an example of such a lane over Midgley way, though I can't remember exactly where now, I stumbled on it while I was out for a walk some years ago; I don't have the mental, or physical energy, for such quests anymore. I'll never know for what real purpose these boundary walls were built, but if I wanted to find oblivion on a winter's night then that's where I should be...frozen in time.

....

OMINOUS DOMINOUS. (BLOKINESS? MAYBE NOT.)

At 82, Charles Bronson is dying of Alzheimer's disease, what an indignity for such a hard man to suffer. I read last week in 'METRO', of 7 men drowning in a vat of blood in a slaughter house in Egypt; 6 of them died trying to save one man who fell in; they use Hal Al methods to kill animals over there, cutting their throats so they'll bleed to death, causing maximum suffering, so I attribute these human deaths to divine justice, ha, ha, ha!!!
I wonder if Otis Redding had a premonition when he was writing and recording 'DOCK OF THE BAY' ('Sittin' on the')? He was killed in a plane crash 3-days after it was released; It should be officially declared the 'losers' anthem, it's been my favourite lonely song, (apart from Jimmy Cliff's 'TOO MANY RIVERS TO CROSS', and 'WHAT BECOMES OF THE BROKEN HEARTED' by.....? [I can't remember his name, and he died this year as well. 6/7/06.]) for the last 30 years or so.
Going back to 'blokiness', I wonder if the high suicide level among young men has got anything to do with the fact that inside, they're not 'mad for it', and see death as the only way out of our macho culture? I know more about 'flip flops' than I do about 'hip hop', and as for 'bling bling'? It doesn't mean a thing to me. The whole hip-hop, bling-bling thing is as alien to me as Islamic Fundamentalism; and quite frankly, just as distasteful, disgraceful, and bad!!!
Will I be spending 'Crimbo' in Spain? I certainly hope so; it might cost me up to £500 but who cares!? It's only money, as that fat bitch of a school headmistress said when she was robbing her school blind of half a million quid. Today, sentencing day, she's scuttled off to hospital, pretending to be ill, the conning CUNT! (22/8/03.)

....

A CANCEROUS SUCCUBUS/INCUBUS.

A cancerous succubus/incubus has an inoperable tumour-like grip on me, it won't be satisfied until I'm dead. By which time my head should be the shape and consistency of a large, rotting pumpkin.

My thyroid isn't shorting out, and I haven't got gout, so whatever it is that ails me, remains strongly in doubt; how about I'm just worn out? The dubious reward of an unrelentingly hard life with very little TLC in it? Well, if that's the case, then let it be; another 40 years of what I've already had doesn't appeal to me. Most cancer victims slip into a coma before they die, like being under a general anaesthetic, which makes death easier to handle; I might even have a smile on my face and be sticking two fingers in the air as a final act of defiance when I get sucked under.

···

Sometimes my penis is like Guy de Bergerak's nose, (I wonder if I'm widely off the mark with that name?). If it scents that there just might be love in the air, it grows long and thick, and dribbles. But alas, like him, I always end up wiping my love snot off its tip after it's had a good sneeze and cleared its passages. AAACCCHHHOOO!!!
Yes, I was a bit wide of the mark with 'Guy', thanks to a radio quiz I've learnt it's Cirano de Berjerak...jack!
I'm attempting to find myself a more useful literary agent, practically the only other one who'll take on poetry apart from 'NEW AUTHORS SHOWCASE'; I'm posting photocopies of my 5 book covers off to her tomorrow. I've had a little glow of warmth in anticipation, tempered by force of habit to expect the worst, like, 'Sorry but our lists are full'.
(The name of that particular publishing agency escapes me, but I did send them a nasty 'Crimbo' card after her snotty rejection letter; anonymously of course.)

···

HELLO AGAIN 'OR'.

I thought that she loved me, but when I made my play, she shoved me away; there wasn't much to say after that so I called her a silly twat and stormed off.
('Or' was the shortened name of a waitress in the 'fun' pub at my hotel in Thailand this year; the above two lines of verse aren't strictly true, but they might as well be.)

···································

SOMEONE GIVE ME AN OUZI SO I CAN BLOW SEVERAL HOLES THROUGH ME VERY QUICKLY.

I met this floozy called Susie, she was very boozy and not very choosy, which suited me because beggars can't be choosers, but desperate people can be users. I made sure I was out of her smelly, moth-eaten dump before we could both wake up and see what washed-up, washed-out frumps we looked in the cold glare of another hung-over day.

....

MATILDA THE HUNTRESS. (SHE'D HAVE MADE ATILLA THE HUN QUAKE WITH HER STEELY GAZE.)

She thought she'd spotted a real wrong 'un when she spotted me, about to make my way through the 'NOTHING TO DECLARE' section at Manchester Airport. Suddenly I was caught up in her nightmare world of, 'You're guilty until you can prove yourself innocent.'
All of five feet tall and three foot round the middle, 'Matilda' began to roast me on her griddle, she went thru' my 'biggies' and then thru' my 'smalls', (there was a rap artist called 'Biggy Smalls' remember? He was shot and killed a few years ago; it took a small crane to hoist his barrel-shaped coffin into his hole in the ground, [not all of that statement is correct by the way]), mentally banging my head up against the wall in her quest to reveal the truth that I was obviously concealing up my back passage.
Only an hour before, I'd been revelling in the discomfiture of two flustered and harassed, would-be passengers at Skipol Airport in Amsterdam, as they ran up and down the departure hall unable to find their exit gate, which they were urgently being called to; they were last seen running off in a lather shouting, 'SHIT, SHIT, SHIT!' Oh how we, smugly settled in our right spot for boarding, laughed (quietly of course), at their expense.
But I wasn't laughing now as 'Matilda' continued to turn my honey-toned tan pale, with her probing questions and fingers; fingers I felt would be only too happy to pull my shit apart, (wearing regulation gloves of course), in an attempt to find condoms full of 'crack' cocaine. Failing that, she could wire my brain up to a lie detector and turn the voltage up to full throttle, until I confessed to being Bin Laden in a Michael Jackson-type facial transformation. But in the end she had to admit defeat and neatly repacked my defiled belongings, but she gave me a look which said, 'I'll get you next time you drugs and goat's meat smuggling terrorist.' I've been having bad dreams ever since.
(Regular readers of my work will have noted by now that I'm not meticulously dating everything I'm putting onto this manuscript; this is

because as it's my last ever collection, and it's called 'ESOTERIC ESPLANADE', I thought I'd try and create an air of mystery around times and dates; only my innermost circle of devotees will ever know the truth...plus my biographer of course.)

....

ALMOST NEARLY REALLY.
(TRULY, MADLY, DEEPLY IT IS NOT.)

Inexplicably, someone's walking about minus £2,600,000, which rightfully belongs to them; unless they died shortly after buying the winning ticket for Lotto Extra, May 10th this year, and ate the said ticket shortly before they died...perhaps even choking on it.

How lackadaisical can you be, not to check your lottery tickets as soon as poss'!? It makes a mockery of those of us who can't win anything, other than a few lousy quid, and who are desperate for a substantial pot so they can flesh out the plot of their otherwise meaningless existences. Whoever bought that ticket has only got till November (2003) to have a brainstorm and remember that they bought it, using their personal set of six lucky numbers based on their own, and their mother's date of birth; after Nov, 10th their claim will be worthless.

It really is intriguing, maybe this absentee winner is going around telling a tale of woe along the lines of nothing ever goes right for them, alienating the few friends they've been able to make, causing them to say, 'Give us a break, leave it out, it's your shout'. My face has adopted a miserable pose through too much thwarted self ambition, my unmade fortune lying between the pages of my undiscovered work; because some jerk of a publisher (quite a few actually) can't see its merits. Who needs publishers anyway? Are they really the arbiters of public taste? More like a waste of vital space and time; they've almost been the death of my will to live and give my all to the creative flow.
Axmus Smoe, aka Phil Fletcher.

....

EVANESCENT FUGACITY. (THE BEAUTIFUL SKY, HEAVEN'S EYE.)

If I could employ all the cerebral loquacity I could muster, (I'm always talking to myself inside my head), or use all the verbal bluff and bluster that poets cryptically rely on, I couldn't do ample justice to the beautiful sky. Yes, it's true the sun lights it up, but even when its incandescent glow is obscured by clouds, acting as shrouds on bleak winter days, its greys can be shot through with silver and violet, especially at dusk, and sometimes you get a roseate hue on the skyline, a rusty pink glow as someone so aptly described it

It's not just the sun that is the life giver for me; it is the panoramic whole of the ephemeral sky that dies at the end of each passing day, only to be reborn the next morning. And nothing we do to the planet can destroy it; we might turn it a fiery red for an aeon or two from the evil that humans do all too depressingly frequently. Even if we destroy the world and all the other innocent (by our standards anyway) life upon it, the sky will still look indifferently down on the Earth below, waiting impassively for life to start growing again, staining the parched dead ground a luscious green after raining 'God's tears' down on it.

Acerbically, it wouldn't bother me if humanity was wiped out by its own stupidity, it would be doing the rest of creation a favour; as long as they're all there to watch me ascend into the rainbow's centre, with my reproving finger pointing down at them, and my frown telling them that 'YOU'RE ALL DOOMED'!!!

(This piece should earn me my place among the 'Gods' on that literary pantheon; I think I'll nominate myself now before posterity can bury me completely.)

....

MY TOP FIVE.
(I've finally realised what my top five favourite things are, I don't know if I can stretch the list to ten.)

 1/ LYING CURLED UP IN BED!!!
2/ EATING TO LIVE, (and preferably enjoying my food.)
3/ READING a relevant book.
4/ WATCHING TV OR LISTENING TO THE RADIO, (the latter preferably in bed.)
5/ FANTASISING ABOUT FINANCIAL SECURITYAWAY FROM STATE BENEFITS.
6/ TRAVEL.
7/ GETTING DISCOVERED.
8/   "   SUCKSEXFULL.

9/ HAVING MY OWN PRIVATE HOUSE AND ACRE OF LAND.
10/ HAVING A BEAUTIFUL AND INTELLIGENT PARTNER A GOOD
DEAL YOUNGER THAN MYSERLF.
11/ COLLECTING CD'S.
12/ CAMPAIGNING TO PARLIAMENT ABOUT ISSUES THAT AFFECT
ME, LIKE THE FEARED AND LOATHED TV LICENCE FOR
INSTANCE.

....

MY PENIS IS A PSYCHIC.

My penis is psychic, 'he's' got a will of his own (geddit?). When he gets the
urge, he's like a dog scenting a bitch on heat, and he would literally drag me
off to wait his chance if either of us knew where the 'lead' was coming from;
so I have a wank and keep 'my money in the bank'. If I took him to a massage
parlour we'd both feel short-changed if some wench jerked him off like she
was pulling an udder.

....

AN IMAGINARY CONVERSATION WITH MY IMAGINARY FRIEND.

'Well, you seem really real to me; I just can't understand why people can't see
in you what I can. A warm, generous nature, a loving manner, and you're
good with a spanner when someone needs sorting out. Talk about vicious! You
levered that geezer's nose right off when he wouldn't pay up the other day;
truly awesome'.

....

'YOU HAVE NO LOVE IN YOUR LIFE'. (Uttered by the same automated
voice that tells you, you have no new messages when you check your
voicemail.)

'You have no love in your life; you can't afford to 'buy' a mail order wife.
Please give up all hope of finding personal happiness…Please hang up'.

(There's an empty silence after you've put down the phone.)

....

TENACITY.

I know we're all afraid of dying, old people more than most, when what they
should be telling themselves is, 'You're history, you're toast!' As I get closer
to joining their swelling ranks, I give no thanks to my so-called maker, who's
taken the piss out of me for most of my mis-shapen life. Only the hale and
hearty should be kept above ground to party, the rest of the moaning clots
should be shown their 'plots' and told to keep quiet...or else.
(Well I ain't hale and hearty no mor;, in a less humane environment I might
be shown that final door, whether I was willing to pass through it or not.)

....

'ENGLAND STINKS LIKE A CHEMICAL LOO'. (Reminiscent of 'ENGLAND SWINGS LIKE A PENDULUM DO, circa 1967.)

'It's a muggers' paradise, criminals with hearts as cold as ice, there's not
much room left for being nice in this land of fucked-up, discontented lice.
Rampant greed might feed your need for material satisfaction, but it won't
satisfy your soul...if you had one to begin with. Better to live without one if
you ask me, if you want to thrive in a predatory world. Or go to the other
extreme, reject materialism and all its ills, fight the good fight with all your
skills and without any allegiance to a religious doctrine, other than
humanitarianism; ('humanism' for short.)
If I didn't feel threatened by the BNP, with whose racist, bigoted policies I
have some sympathy, I'd feel free to carry on being ME! An unfettered
thinker, in a stinker of a country.
(Is it my fault that I prefer white people to black? It's genetic Jack; I would
like to send the majority back from whence they came and close the door on
our insane asylum (political) policy. So if this ever comes to light, all those
right on, Negro-shagging, 'pinko' lefties will be screaming for my blood, that's
good, I've got eight pints they can have.)

....

I'M AN EMOTIONAL KLEPTOMANIAC.

Just a voice in a room on a CD, singing breathily and earthily, 'Come away with me', and where she leads I would gladly follow; for her heart is full and hollow like a cactus tree, she's so busy being free.
When I was young I obeyed the call of 'The Blind Owl' and 'The Bear' and went on the road, again and again; hitching a ride in the rain or walking along a deserted highway as the birds piped in the early dawn; one time I bedded down on a 'lawn' at the side of a busy road, only one driver stopped to make sure I wasn't dead.
But my wanderings never led me anywhere where I could stay, except sitting on the dock of the bay on my own, and this loneliness wouldn't leave me alone.
There's an old song by Mel Torme, one of the few mainstream hits that came his way called, 'I'M COMIN' HOME', that I really like; well wherever I lay my woolly hat, be it flat, bungalow, or 3-storey house, that's my home. The only problem is, people won't leave me alone to enjoy the starry, starry night; like Vincent I have to endure the plight/blight of living with the common people.
It's in the area of love that I've been left most alone, 10,000 light years away from my heart's desire; c'mon baby light my fire in this arctic waste, my name's Major Tom, what's yours? Oh, Pretty Woman? No, you're not interested? It worked for Roy, the sad boy, Orbison. Ah, but if you could see my eyes so green, they're the greenest green you've ever seen, flashing bright emerald with envy whenever a happy family group draws near; a ripple of fear passes over their grave. I am the howling wolf that whines in the night, don't you ever kiss me once, kiss me twice, treat me nice because this is the end, beautiful friend, the end of madness and street lights, the end of nights where I tried to kill myself with booze and pills; it's cheap thrills living for me from now on. It's alright ma, it's only me bleeding loneliness from every pore, but no more dead heroes anymore, you'll always find me out to lunch at the dark end of the street, snapping my fingers and shuffling my feet to the beat-beat of the tom-toms through the jungle traffic's roar with a rebel yell, crying more, more, more! And if you won't do it my way you're a whore, whore, whore!
So please close the blue velvet door and push the key to my heart through the windmills of my mind; true love's too hard to find.

(This is another piece [which I'd completely forgotten I'd written] that I can die a happier man, knowing I've penned it. It compares favourably, in a rap style, to the kind of angst-ridden rubbish I heard on Radio 4's 'SPOKEN WORD' poetry prog' the other night. 6/7/06.)

....

ANTI ART, ANTI MUSIC, ANTI HUMOUR, ANTI LIFE.

Somehow, the ID has developed an IQ and an ego, and has been made manifest, strutting around on its hind legs, defying sweet reason to try and suss out what the hell's really going on in the 'creative' world.
The new music, mainly Hip-Hop, (not to be confused with Flip-Flop which is one half of a pair of slip on sandals), is only for the spiritually damned and those who have a discordant ear; and as for avant garde classical? I wouldn't go anywhere near it, unless I was dragged there...kicking and screaming! !!!
(This is an update, I heard an item about Tom Waits on THE TODAY programme today on Radio4, this pretentious oaf is doing one performance in London; tickets sold out in 29 minutes, leaving 150,000 masochists unable to get any; this wanker has been labelled the spokesperson for the lonely and broken hearted!! That's my fucking job!! At least I can inject some humour into my pathos; him!? Have any of you heard his so-called 'music'!? It's excruciatingly painful even in short bursts. I think he should be conscripted and sent to Iraq, and his audience along with him, the bunch of arseholes. 4/11/04.)
Modern art stands apart from the norm, human heads made out of frozen human blood, human corpses reactivated by impregnating them with a type of plastic resin, and set in all manner of hellish poses; one exhibit is a monstrous man on a monstrous horse which looks like something out of the film version of THE DEVIL RIDES OUT. And then there's the infamous 'Unmade Bed' and animals cut in half; all this surmounted by a mound of junk, (quite literally), has taken a large chunk out of Paul Saatchi's misbegotten millions; I'd say he's been taken to the cleaners and bled dry. (Another update, earlier this year a lot of his crap went up in flames in a warehouse fire, so there is divine intervention after all.)
Nowadays you have to brace yourself for the worst where 'new' humour's concerned, how unshockable can you be before your stomach's turned to a heaving mass of nausea?. 'I say, I say, I say, I saw you trying to sneak out while I wasn't looking, you fucking mard-arses. Too strong for you is it?' And that to the ghosts of Eric Morecambe, Ernie Wise, and Tommy Cooper, who

stand at the back of these 'comedy' venues with looks of tortured surprise and disgust; they don't understand these savage tirades of malice and lust; or if they do they know only too well that the surest road to Hell is lined with the decimated ranks of unfunny comedians. (Only yesterday I left a stinging rebuke on Channel 4's website about 'GREEN WING', describing it as 'the most embarrassing pile of excrement ever shown on British TV, toe curlingly cringe making' etc, and signing my hate email: Mangas Colorados, deceased. 5/10/04.)

And lastly I come to the anti life force that is everywhere, (and spreading rapidly), trying to oppress me permanently into a state of despair and ennui, and except on my good days, succeeding too; every day can be a blue Monday if I let it. This blight is driven mainly by men in cars, they turn into Satan's slaves in this, the Devil's own invention; blaring horns and gunning motors, I've had much more than my quota of this form of torture. And blended in with barking dogs and car alarms, this rural idyll's lost its charms for me. I stay here because I realistically can't afford to move, and anyway wherever I go this evil follows me. (As witnessed in my latest piece called 'THE DANCE OF THE SUGAR PLUM ELEPHANTS', referring to the school of theatre dance above my head, 5 nights a week and all day Saturday; another 'fine mess' my perverse fate has got me into, and another manifestation [infestation more like] of anti art.)

....

I'M A SAINT JOHN'S WORT CONVERT...ME.

The European Union is seeking to greatly interfere in the way we buy our vitamins, minerals, and alternative medicines here in the disunited kingdom, (we haven't even got a 'king'!) An Industry that has a 1.5 billion pound a year turnover; and I fear that the lily-livered powers that be here will let them have their autocratic way. I recently wrote to Holland & Barrett, a leading manufacturer of vitamins and minerals, voicing my concerns about this threat from Brussels; pointing out how I thought it should be conventional medicines that need to be under closer scrutiny because of the unpleasant side effects a lot of them contain. H & B wrote back, more or less saying they shared my concerns, but feared that the EU are going to steam roller any opposition to their plans to drastically reduce the potency of the vitamins and minerals we're allowed to buy in Britain; a good enough reason on its own for us to pull out of the increasing nightmare that is the EC, controlled by France and Germany.

My most recent experience of unpleasant side effects from prescribed medication, was from a urinary product called 'FLO MAX', that was supposed to help ease a swollen prostate gland, improve urine flow, and relieve the stinging pain that goes with this problem. I paid £6.30p for 30 capsules. Fortunately I was able to get hold of a slim volume about the prostate gland and all the things that can go wrong with it. It also listed treatments, including my medication and its possible side effects; one of these was retrograde ejaculation. If I hadn't been forewarned about this, I'd have had a pretty nasty shock when forced to masturbate to get some sexual relief, about two weeks into the treatment. At the climax there was this sinking feeling and virtually nothing came out; to add insult to my injured libido the other symptoms didn't improve much either, even after another £6.30p's worth of 'FLO MAX'.

Fortunately for me, some months earlier I'd looked up the word/term 'Prostatodynia' on the internet, being long convinced that I had this condition; the site also listed 'Prostatitis'. It listed the results of trials of pollen extract to relieve symptoms, I did mention this to my doctor but he didn't seem impressed. After the retrograde ejaculation scare I decided to try it and eventually tracked down a product called 'POLLEN B' from a health food shop. And hey, guess what? It actually made a big improvement, and I could wank myself off with renewed vigour; there's also Saw Palmetto which works out more expensive if prostatitis is a recurring problem, like in my case.

Due to my impoverished, isolated and lonely situation, I often lose the will to keep my existence going; in the past I've tried prescribed anti depressants with horrific results; the last one was 'SEROXAT' which sent me down into Hell while I was on it. Fuck knows what they put into that stuff, but it's a killer; I came off it before it destroyed me. (There's an ongoing debate about the merits or otherwise of this widely used drug, some of us should never take it because it has an adverse effect on our metabolisms; it's a chemical cosh for us to beat ourselves to death with, if we're not careful.)

When all the positive publicity surrounding 'PROZAC' came out I was tempted to try it, but my previous experiences put me off, because there were those who'd suffered similar experiences to me on PROZAC, when I was on SEROXAT; (even the name sounds sinister doesn't it, like DALEK). Luckily I'd heard that St John's Wort is called Nature's Prozac, but the cost of it had always put me off trying it. Last August, H & B had a special offer on St John's Wort, and being sick of feeling suicidal most of the time, I decided to try it. It was with some trepidation that I swallowed my first capsule, but apart from some drowsiness I felt no ill effects.

The recommended dosage was 3 capsules a day, but the drowsiness was a nuisance, so I switched to taking two before I went to bed, and I'm very pleased to say that the effects have been nothing but beneficial. I've even been dreaming vividly again, those ancient herbalists certainly knew a thing or two didn't they? (It must have all been trial and error, I wonder if they tried stuff out on animals first, like deadly nightshade for instance?) And believe me, living where I do, amongst some of the most depressing creatures in England, you need all the medical help you can get, off prescription of course; and even tho' I've moved from the Todmorden situation, I'm still not free from oppression; it comes in all guises, and I don't care who you are, I'd like to see you go a week in my current situation without resorting to something for your nerves and well-being; living in a flat beneath a dance school is not for the faint-hearted or those of a low tolerance level...I'm suffering accordingly.

HORN TO BE WILD.

British drivers are the least horny in Europe. They rarely use their car hooters and almost never beep at night or early in the morning, according to a poll published today by roadside restaurants chain LITLE CHEF.
Some drivers say they never ever use them and, if called to do so, would have a problem 'remembering which button to push'. Some drivers consider it 'too aggressive' – even though they admit to sometimes shouting at their fellow motorists. More than 2,500 drivers were quizzed. The worst horn hooters are in Italy. Second in the survey was Spain, then France. 17/8/03.

Once again this place is the exception to the apparent rule, car horn honking/hooting is rife here, much to my annoyance and discomfiture; and you wonder why I don't believe in God!? I don't believe in anything except surviving against hopeless odds; to keep sticking the finger up to adversity as long as my head can hold out without bursting open from too much pressure. The above cutting is taken from THE DAILY STAR on Sunday; I've had 3 CDs from this august publication in the last 8 days, can't be bad can it, ay?

....

THE ULTIMATE LOSER'S TOP TEN. (The order they're played in doesn't really mater.)

1/ WHEN WILL I BE LOVED? The Everley Brothers.
2/ I AM A ROCK. Simon & Garfunkel.
3/ SOUNDS OF SILENCE   *   *
4/ SISTERS OF MERCY. Leonard Cohen.
5/ SPIRIT IN THE SKY. Norman Greenbaum.
6/ I DON'T LIVE TODAY. Jimi Hendrix.

7/ TOO MANY RIVERS TO CROSS. Jimmy Cliff.
8/ DOCK OF THE BAY. Otis Redding.
9/ NOBODY CARES FOR ME. Arthur Lee & LOVE.
10/ BLACK SHEEP. SRC (LP version.)
(Nobody cares about me; only me; and not all of the time either; sometimes I hate myself.)

....

I MIGHT NOT HAVE HAD MY FAIR SHARE OF SEX, BUT I'VE MADE UP FOR THAT IN DREAMING AND SCHEMING ABOIUT HOW TO GET MY LEG OVER ANYTHING OITHER THAN THE SIDE OF THE BED.

When I've been battered down too often by adversity, the real me tends to fade away and be replaced by a sad and grim-faced effigy; but like the phoenix, my effigy is burnt to ashes periodically and the real me re-emerges for a while; I always know when I'm back, things get done with renewed vigour.
My latest return was triggered after one of the worst bouts of acid reflux I can remember suffering, late last Saturday night; and to add insult to injury, I had ice cold feet as well. It was a weekend of heavy frost up here on the side of the valley slope (21/1/04). I'd reverted to my old habit of opening a bottle of wine on a Saturday night, having got away with a liberal intake of cheap wine while I was in Paris over Xmas; Paris at this time of year is special, especially for lovers in love, I wasn't unfortunately, as per usual, but maybe this Yuletide coming…? (The prospects are looking decidedly bleak.) They must spend millions of Euros on coloured lights; the effect is truly romantic.
So yes, I cracked open a bottle of Argentinean dry white, the grapes nurtured at the feet of the Andes Mountains, very aromatic. I didn't guzzle it, I drank it over a period of 3-hours while watching TV; there were 2 new comedies on BBC2: 'GRASS' and 'STILL GAME', and a 'new' film called 'RAVENOUS', that didn't live up to expectations. There was a long sketch in 'STILL GAME' about old Scottish people fiddling the 'leccy', that I thought was really funny.
After 'RAVENOUS' failed to keep me glued to my seat, (it was full of gratuitous gory violence which I'm sick of), I turned to ITV 1's 1960 offering: 'THE UNFORGIVBEN', starring Burt Lancaster and Audrey Hepburn; a rambling saga about racist bigotry in the old west. Audrey was supposed to be a Kiowa Indian girl brought up by Burt's family, and the Kiowa's wanted her back.
I finished off my palatable bottle of wine about 1.15am, just as Kiowa braves were committing suicide by riding into a hail of bullets; so much for Native

American savvy. I wasn't up for this needless slaughter so I went to bed. There had been a few twinges of protest from my stomach as the wine was going down, but no indication of what was to come. I don't know how long I slept before burning acid indigestion woke me up, and kept me awake for the most of the rest of the night. I was too distressed to think of going to put a pair of thick socks on, to try and warm my feet; I can only liken the pain in my digestive tract to that which swallowing some bleach might incur, truly horrendous. I took a couple of St John's Wort capsules to ease my mental and physical agony about 8 am, Sunday morning; I then dozed fitfully for a couple of hours.

So when I surfaced, I can't remember what time it was, but it was a lot earlier than I'd anticipated getting up, I had not only a hangover to deal with, but the residual pain of the acid reflux attack as well. It eventually dawned on me to try an Evening Primrose Oil capsule to relieve my digestive discomfort, and it did start to gradually ease the pain. The first thing I did after my meagre breakfast, was to take the sheets and pillowcases off the bed; it'd been nearly a month since I'd changed them, though in my defence I had been away over C/mas and the New Year. I find that our intense cold snaps make everything feel grubby, so they went in the washing machine, along with my musty pyjamas. I had quite a busy day lined up, washing clothes and bathing myself. As the fug in my head began to clear I realised I wasn't making the most out of my savings, so I set about getting my brain to work even more effectively by figuring out a complicated transaction which involved filling in forms, (if you've ever felt as rough as I did last Sunday, you'll appreciate that even putting the washer on a 40-degree wash programme was complicated); I hope the DSS never read this for 'complicated' reasons.

It was while I was struggling over my form-filling that I realised I was on my reincarnation from my most recent effigy burning; I could feel my confidence and determination rising like new sap from the ashes. It's been four days now and I'm still on the up, even though I'm under constant psychic surveillance and attack from the mutants of the cursed earth; aka the residents (some, not all) of the Ashenhurst estate. Things do come in threes, good or bad, I lost a fiver on last Saturday's rollover lotto draw, netting not even a tenner out of it, but I know people lose a lot more than that, the silly fuckers, it serves them right! So I lost a fiver, had really bad acid reflux, and freezing cold feet; enough to wipe the synthetic smile off anyone's face. But am I downhearted? Am I fuck! I'm still dreaming (wanking actually) about an impossible liaison with a young lady who shall remain nameless and unidentifiable to future biographers.

(I'm upgrading my psychic attackers to 'she devils/Satan's bitches and dark forces in general; though as I often say to them, 'You're bigger losers than I could ever be, wasting your time targeting a 57-year-old man with disabilities, and no money to speak of'. I ask you, who but the biggest retard on the planet would waste their psychic energy thus? It's just my luck to be pursued by an anally retentive shit-for-brains dummy).9/10/04.)

....

FRIEND OR FIEND? PLEASE STATE WHICH ONE YOU ARE BY TICKING THE ALL IMPORTANT 'R'. IF YOU DON'T KNOW, YOU CAN GO BELOW UNTIL YOU DO

For some mildly dyslexic reason I was spelling 'friend' as 'fiend' yesterday at Halifax library while putting work on disc, and the machine wasn't dishing out red lines to indicate a spelling error like it usually does; I think a certain fat cunt whose name I can't even remember for certain, may have tampered with it, and who I would classify as mildly fiendish and annoying; she's got indefinable mental health problems. I just wish she wouldn't come in while I'm there because I more than mildly hate her, which isn't fair because if she was more than halfway decent-looking, she'd stand a fighting chance of getting into my good books. (Like this one for instance that I'm putting on disc for future self-publication…maybe.)

....

IT'S OKAY TO BE MISERABLE IN KWIKSAVE, EVERYBODY ELSE IS.

I wonder who it was who took the philosophic decision to set up KWIKSAVE? It seems to have been a thankless task, as the supermarket chain lurches from financial crisis to financial crisis. And yet KWIKSAVE is a good place to shop. I reckon I'm about £3 a week better off than if I had to do all my shopping at SAFEWAY nee MORRISONS, for example.
Whenever I use 'my' local KWIKSAVE I feel tense, this could be because they employ mainly young Asian males to fill shelves and sometimes work on the tills; there's still this male pride issue to deal with; I don't feel like a complete man because I do my own shopping, they might be feeling vulnerable because they work in a shop; not the best image for a young man's sense of machismo I suppose.
Even though there are always bargains on offer, customers in general seem to be miserable; do they feel self conscious because shopping at KWIKSAVE implies that you're poor or a member of the 'under' class? Or are they merely

peeved that they've got to pay anything at all for their grub? New managers don't seem to last long, their initial enthusiasm soon gets sapped at the Todmorden branch. I wish I could be a manager there, I'd be telling everyone to cheer up or go and shop at NETTO in Halifax.

At our local KWIKSAVE, the same extremely rotund (does that mean round?) woman has been on the checkout for the last 18 years; the most conversation we've exchanged, on my part is, 'Have they nicked all the baskets again?' 'Yes', and 'thank-you.' Some years ago a young girl worked on the checkouts there, and for some inscrutable reason she took a fancy to me; but the snob in me didn't like her accent, and I'd set my sights on one of my lost causes, so much so that I came close to topping myself when she inevitably rejected me; so I froze Miss KWIKSAVE out. I have deep regrets about that, if only we could have met in another setting, and if only my eyesight was a hell of a lot better so I could have some real control over my life…………

....

BADLY RE-HUNG DOORS.

I do have a sneaking curiosity about how the re-formed DOORS concert went last December in Leeds or Sheffield. I can't remember the name of the venue, (it was Wembley Arena, I've just checked.) For a start they were only a trio this time, 2 of the originals and Ian Astbury of THE CULT fame (or was it cunt brain?). Quite possibly there's a feature article about it on the net? I hate wallowing in nostalgia, and I hate so-called 'tribute groups', parasitic leeches would be a more appropriate description; and most of all I hate the idiots and morons who go to these gigs hoping to relive their lost youth. I wonder if Jim Morrison would be happy to be a caricature of his former self, like Mick Jagger and Keith Richards for instance?

....

THE ENIGMA CLUB.

I am the DJ at The Enigma, The Psychedelic Music Appreciation Society: (PMAS.) Biology and evil psychology don't mix; suicide bombers go straight to HELL!!…IN PIECES!

There's a wide-awake wet dream scene going on in my pants and my head every time I come away from spending some time with…discretion is the better part of valour; it's an impossible scenario even by today's hazy standards. Maybe one day we'll meet up in Pattaya and I'll take her straight to bed in my condo. Meanwhile, it's solo sex in the mind and body for me, what a waste of a lovely primal urge.

....

FALSE MODESTY.

Last week at some ghastly pop music awards fest in America, Janet Jackson's right tit popped out, a 'wardrobe malfunction' as it's now being called. This minor sensation attracted 200,000 e-mails of complaint, and in a daily tabloid paper I bought last Saturday, I read that some woman had launched a multi billion dollar law suit for distress and trauma caused by this heinous offence; I put all this over-reaction down to hysterical hypocrisy. Do all these complainants take a bath wearing a blindfold and surgical gloves? How would they have reacted to Johnny Rotten saying, 'You fucking cunts', live on TV last Tuesday night on 'I'M A CELEBRITY, GET ME OUT OF HERE', which only attracted 91 complaints to 'OFCOM'? (I saw a photo of that offending breast in the same paper; it looked like an elbow sticking out of her covered chest; not very appetising at all by my standards.)

....

FRUSTRATED AMBITION.

The fact that I'm a low, or non-achiever, niggles and gnaws away at me like a dog worrying a bone to get at the marrow, or a rat scraping away at the side of a coffin to get at the corpse inside. Yet there's nothing I can do about this unfortunate state of affairs; all my efforts to change my fate come to nothing. So this self-torture is just one more burden I have to bear, it's not fair. I'd rather my mind remained a comparative blank, and let me get on in dull resignation, with the business of day-to-day living on a fixed income; maintaining my motto that, 'THE LONGER I LIVE THE MORE I CAN ACHIEVE'; impaired health permitting. (The situation hasn't changed 3-years on, I still feel this way; all my attempts to escape this negative side of my parallel world have failed; it could be 2008 before I'm finally free from the dark side for good.)

....

MY YEAR OF DESPERATELY TRYING TO GET DISCOVERED...WITHOUT SUCCESS OF COURSE

In 2003 I pulled out all the stops to put the most recent of my modern poetry collections together; bringing the total of self published works to five, plus a sixth which is on disc and which I have a single copy of, printed out; it keeps growing all the time. I paid £50 for a page on a poetry website, and I set up a writers group at PLATFORM ONE in Todmorden; I even alerted all major poetry publishers to my web page by sending detailed post cards to them, the end result? Nothing! No response whatsoever! So what else am I supposed to do, make a public protest like those fathers seeking better access rights to their kids?
(I still hold out a faint glimmer of hope in this year's Bridport Arts Centre Poetry Prize [2004], the results of which should be out sometime in November.) (That faint glimmer was cruelly snuffed out, but undaunted, I've entered 'POETRY IS DEAD!' into this year's Bridport Arts Poetry Comp', as I've already mentioned; I could desperately do with the £5000 1st prize money. I should win, but the English poetry scene is dominated by these tenacious anal retentives like AN Wilson, (I don't know if he writes poetry, but after reading an article by him in last Saturday's Daily Mail about BIG BROTHER on C4, I'm mightily relieved he's not the judge in the poetry comp'; he should be positioned at the Gates of Hell, pointing at the entrance sign: 'LEAVE ALL HOPE YOU WHO IN HERE ENTER'. As it is, you lose all hope after reading the Daily Mail. PLF, 7/7/06.)

....

LET THE ICE CAPS MELT.

('What is ice, snow and tempest good for? Absolutely nothin' y'all'.) The cold, and the extreme cold, serve no purpose; it is anti productive and anti life, as far as we're concerned anyway; it kills or debilitates. How much ecological damage would really be done if both the polar ice caps melt? Think of all the land it will free up for our ever expanding global population; the ever

encroaching deserts will become green and verdant again, it will literally create a whole new world; maybe sea water will become less salty.
If a few million, or even a billion people get drowned living in coastal regions, it won't matter (except to them); we've got plenty left to replace them with...roll on summer!

....

THE POWER BUSINESS. (WIELDING IT, NOT SUPPLYING IT.)

Our prime minister now earns £179,000 a year (in 2003); that's rather modest considering what other captains of industry (UK, PLC) screw out of their companies, and they don't have life or death making decisions to take either. I've watched our current PM turn from a fairly young-looking man into an old man, in the space of seven years. He's gone from being revered to almost being reviled, by a weak willed and skittish populace; mainly over Iraq. He might bounce back, I don't know. He's a fan of the euro and I'm not. After my recent visits to Europe I've decided it's a great big rip off, a lot like modern day living, the world over.
(Tony's just had his second heart op'; not that I resent him having it, he's a damned hard working politician, and despite the fact that everyone else in British politics is rapidly backtracking on Iraq, saying we shouldn't have gone to war, etc, Mr Blair is standing firm, not willing to 'apologise' for removing Saddam the Impaler on a flimsy pretext. I'm a hardliner too; I think we should forcibly deport those eight muslim terrorist suspects being held indefinitely in Belmarsh Prison...)

....

HI! I'M BIG BAD BILLY GOAT GRUFFY, (as in 'BUFFY' the vampire shagger) THE 'HEX' AND 'SEX VAMPIRE' SLAYER.

At nearly 57, and being uncomfortably realistic, my life has no meaning except to myself; ergo, shouldn't I in all decency, go and throw myself under a train? Apart from the horrendous pain I could incur from this rash act, it's a fact that almost certainly my body would be rent asunder, leaving my severed head a long way from my scattered feet. The railway police are allowed two hours to clear a body off the tracks and make a report.

I've heard the retort, 'It smells like the meat counter in a butcher's', well they haven't smelt my insides, which is more like when the tide's coming in with a layer of untreated sewage on top. I should stop this introspective speculation, but before I do I wonder if you have time for a final ejaculation before you're torn apart by the 9.52am train from Halifax to Todmorden?

You can't go against your fate, and mine's been totally evil so far; I'd need to be Houdini to escape it, (before his untimely demise of course, due to a stunt going wrong), climbing higher through hoops of fire on a unicycle, facing the wrong way, year after year, day after day, just to keep the hex monsters at bay; as for the sex vampires? I don't know why they hang around me, I've not had sex since 1983, unless you count a shag I paid for in the 21st century.

....

THE RICH MAN'S GETTING MORE THAN HIS FAIR SHARE OF DESPERATE DAN'S POOR COW PIE.

I know all about desperation, me, buying a few lotto tickets (the most I've bought for a single draw at one time is £5's worth) can act like respiration on a soul starved of hope, and gagging for a means of escape from a poisonous atmosphere. But now, living on a modest fixed income, I realise I'm behaving like a dope; I'm already £16 down this year. At 28 pence from each ticket sold going to 'good causes', that's £4.48p I've tipped up, at least if I'd gone into a charity shop I'd have got something back for that tiny sum; possibly a woolly scarf and a woolly hat.

Various scandals have broke before about lottery money going to feed the ravening maw of various national institutions; the first was 13 million quid for the 'Churchill Papers., (how many were there of them?), Then there was the national opera, the theatre and the arts; these cash guzzling tarts can cut capers round us lesser mortals when it comes to getting their wicked way.

I'd consider it an act of aural torture to go and listen to a play sung to music by a bunch of overweight, caterwauling hags. And as for the arts? You can shove the Tate Modern as far up your arse as it will go, that might be a show worth seeing. I'm going to exercise my will of iron resolve, no more lotto tickets for me…until next 'saterdee neet' anyway.

....

I'D RATHER EAT A FULL BAR OF TOBLERONE THAN HAVE A TESTOSTERONE IMPLANT ANY DAY.

Testosterone is the hormone traditionally held to be the preserve of the male of the species, not any more. More and more women are muscling in and muscling up. In a programme I saw about it recently, a doctor said too high an intake of it could leave a woman with a clitoris as long as a little finger; he didn't say if this would occur only when the woman became aroused, or whether this thing was permanently going to be hanging down between her legs?

I'm intrigued, I'd love to meet a woman with a clit' like a little penis so I could suck it like a little cock. I suppose some guys who only have little thin dicks would jump at the chance of a big testosterone fix, in the hope it would make their 'members' grow. Mine's so big, thick and hard, it practically glows in the dark when I'm wanking it. It's a waste of a powerful erection when I'm forced to do it by myself; but I've been on the shelf so long my 'past my sell by date' has come round twice. Not very nice for a full-blooded male waiting to exhale in a long gasp of pleasure, just after I've come in a hot wet juicy glory hole.

I'd love to get to grips with some testosteroned-up babe before I'm too old to do her justice 3 to 5 times a night; her unsightly clit' getting in the way of my thrusting cock; of course, if she could grow one about 2 feet long, I could suck it while I was fucking her.

....

THE SUN WENT BEHIND A CLOUD.

The sun went behind a cloud and the light and heat went out, then I became instantly depressed; another winter's afternoon is dragging by while I've got my nose stuck in one more interminable book to help me pass the time. I'm reading a biography about Charles Bukowski, the American existentialist poet and writer, a man after my own heart. I might never have heard of Bukowski if, in the mid nineties, someone who read one of my pieces asked me if I'd heard of him? I said no, but decided to check his writing out; I've read enough now to know that I might be his English counterpart; some people nearly have a heart attack when they see the cover of my 'COPING WITH MADNESS' collection. And if you talk or write about erections and ejaculations or oral sex, they think you've put a hex on them in the hysterically hypocritical atmosphere we're living in now; it's a sin to be masculine in anything other than a new mannish way. After all, women like to have men they can control, which is a dangerous role to play; there're over 100 murder victims of domestic violence in this country every year alone; that says there's something risky about long term relationships. I'd rather kiss the sweet lips of romance as long as they're fresh, fuck the mesh of a stale entanglement.

Charles Bukowski created a persona of a foul mouthed, treacherous, lecherous drunk; those who he betrayed likening him to that smelly skunk, Pierre Le Phew!! But what struck me was his tenacity to his calling as a writer. Relentlessly sending work out to magazines across America at a time when his brand of raw, stark poetry was totally untried; he died a successful man of 74 in 1994; (I've only got 18 years to go to outlive him.)

There's a better tradition of free speech in the States than there is here, and he, like me, hated the establishment of safe, obscure poetry, the milieu of intellectual snobs. I'd rather be like a football yob and batter people over the head with what I have to say; I'm gobbing on the forces of repression. If I want to call 'gays' 'dirty arse-shagging bastards', I'll fucking well do so! No-one can tell me that black is white, that same sex 'sex' is right. It's a blight on human sexuality, they're all wired up the wrong way, sing if you're sad to be gay. I fear that too many poetry mag's are too puffy for my taste; if their titles are anything to go by. I'll try sending two of my self published collections to REBEL INC, the people who've published; LOCKED IN THE ARMS OF A CRAZY LIFE, THE TITLE OF Bukowski's biog' (No luck there either.) My writing is my 'wife', seeing as how I can't find a lover to save my life.

···

ESOTERIC ESPLANADE.

Anyone who's heard 'Nico' singing 'DESERT SHORE' off her LP of the same name, (a haunting, otherworldly, esoteric lyric accompanied by instrumentation straight out of the 'mystery trend'), will know what I mean. I'd like to found a poetry magazine called 'Esoteric Esplanade', and be paid for submissions I accepted. After all, I would have overheads to pay, printing costs being my biggest outlay, and then there's the cost of publicity and distribution; how do I get a good combination of them both? The world's full of failed attempts at finding fortune and fame; to be the name on everyone's lips is my desire, that way I might set smouldering young women's loins on fire; black or yellow haired beauties whose love wouldn't become a funeral pyre...too soon.

(Who'd have thought that on that bleak winter night of 20/2/04, I'd create a short piece that would go on to become the title of this, my seventh, and last collection? I do have an idea for a cover design but I'm not even going to print this work off unless I ever get a genuine offer to publish it. I'm going over to Leeds on Thursday to try and attract the attention of Felix Dennis, the publishing magnate turned poet; he's stinking rich. The way my luck is, I'm not holding out too much hope. 19/10/04.) (Update: I drank enough of his overpriced French wine to feel rather drunk, and listened to enough of his verbal guff to know that if I didn't leave before the second set started, I'd be heckling or booing him; fortunately I had someone with me who used to be a mate, now I think we hate each other; without this much needed extra pair of eyes, I don't think I'd have found Leeds Railway Station unaided, let alone the right platform. And, contrary to my own belief at this time, I've managed to squeeze an eighth collection out of my tortured psyche, a pursuit that's been 'LONELIER THAN DEATH'.   8/7/06.)

....

DARK FORCES, EVIL SOURCES.

A picture jumped off my wall tonight, it was firmly secured with 'BLUTAC'; it's not the first time this has happened, it's a bit annoying but I don't mind. What's worse is the curse someone's trying to impose on my work with Microsoft Windows. It's only word processing that I'm doing, but dark forces using evil sources, are trying to ruin my chances of completion; and I've still got masses to do; lots of old work, and now this new stuff to put on floppy disc. A low risk business you may well think, but my hands and eyes are on the blink. Why does this evil not want me to succeed? Doesn't it like what I'm saying?

....

MY SPERM DON'T COUNT.
(D'yer gerrit? Sperm? Count ? Yer Cunt!)

My services have never been required; I've never squired a lady into the pudding club. I've got it into my head that any offspring sired by me would be deformed hideously. A Cyclops with a big chin and broken nose wouldn't look good in ribbons and bows. But hey! Who wants kids once the novelty's worn off? Horrible sulky things as devious as Lady Luck; especially girls when they're old enough to start fucking, and mummy and daddy still think that butter wouldn't melt in their sneaky little gobs, (only the tumescent knobs of pimply teenage boys would melt in their mouths after they've shot their smelly loads.)

It looks like I'll have to go on raising welts on my bell end from too much horny handed abuse. If I had serious money I could get girls to call me honey, and if I was in Thailand they'd likely mean it too. At the rate I'm going I'll be 65 before I can realise my dream of marriage to a black-haired oriental beauty; and even then I wouldn't be well-heeled enough to do my duty by her. I won't be able to bring her back here, not that I'd want to.

At 57 I still feel intrinsically young, I'm tall with a full head of hair and my own teeth, I no longer mix beneath myself if you know what I mean; no sitting in pubs or haunting singles clubs, (where are they?), no desperately seeking sexual satisfaction; if I want any action I 'bash the bishop', or have a quick fifty off the wrist.

....

DE JA VU, 1, 2, 3& 4, AND MAYBE MORE.

Yeah, born under a bad sign, blah, blah, blah! The unfairness of fate, etc, etc, etc, but in my case it's true, de ja vu, 1, 2, 3 &4, and maybe more-so. Horrible situations recurring repeatedly, and never a sign of it ending; I'm a virtual recluse now, by choice as much as anything else. I'm sick of walking out into a minefield of hate and animosity in this warped community of the upper Calder Valley. I've got my name down for a top floor flat in a tower block in central Halifax, on the quiet side away from the traffic; so that if I ever feel like throwing myself out of the fourteenth floor window, I shouldn't get run over by any passing vehicles, except maybe a 'mum' haring along the pavement pushing a double buggy; they can move at a fair lick, and they don't stop or move out the way for anyone….THE CUNTS!

Once installed in my eyrie, I'll only venture out to go to the shops and the library's ACCESS ROOM. The people who work there are the only people I see; apart from the strangers who constantly come into my range of vision and hearing. 18 years ago I came to Hebden Bridge with 'nothing'; since then I've moved six times to get away from a poisonous atmosphere and vicious people; maybe this year will be the year of the eighth time lucky, and I can get on with the final dull chapters of my life, free of strife. (No such fucking luck!!!!!!!!!!!!!!!!!!! I ended up in a flat with a dance school on top of me; if that wasn't a strong hint for me to go down to the station and throw myself under a train, I don't know what is! But I'm here for the long haul unless I die of ennui and lassitude combined.

ADULATION.

I want some before the PC scum decree it forever incorrect for dissenting voices to be anything other than shunned; seeing as how we can no longer burn dissenters at the stake or torture confessions out of them, not physical torture anyway. I wonder what goes on in the darkest recesses of the heads of the hard line politically correct? Do they allow themselves to mentally say 'Christmas' instead of 'Happy Holiday'? 'Short-arsed runt' instead of 'vertically challenged'? 'Blind fucker' instead of 'severely visually impaired'? Like Bob Dylan's song, 'POSITIVELY 4th St.' says, 'Why don't you just come out once and scream it'? Then I could have something on them and their ice-cold hearts.

Reading about an ugly old wart hog like Charles Bukowski breaking hearts back in the 1970s, and even turning away 'too much pussy', makes me feel lusty for success in this emotionally repressed country of mine; where I've been turned down by everyone from Faber & Faber, to The Pen Press (a vanity publisher); my life's a mess of other people's making. But I'm not quaking anymore, I've survived too much for that, a cabal of silly twats has tried to destroy me and my sanity, but like old JC (was he anti PC or pro? He didn't like moneylenders in the temple y'know), I'm back from the dead, give me an AK47 Ma, I'm really seething.

(Update. I reckon 'New Labour' are like the PC Brigade, having both a public and private persona; they pay lip service to 'socialism' [knowing what I know now about the human condition, I wouldn't even do that], but privately they've all got their snouts in the trough. I reckon 'political correctness' is one huge piss-take by a bunch of cynical manipulators, who are as corrupt and two-faced as your average Christian 'born again' Fundamentalist. 8/7/06.)

....

I'VE ALWAYS HAD DIFFICULTY PEEING.

The prostate gland is situated about 2 inches up inside the bung hole, it's the homo erotic person's pleasure zone, and doctor's have to insert a finger into your rectum to check its size and shape; it's a horrible experience if you're not 'gay'. I've endured it 3 or 4 times now, but have vowed 'never again'. It isn't very painful unless your prostate's swollen and inflamed, like mine has been in the past, it's just uncomfortable and humiliating. It's a bit like when you stick your finger down your throat to make yourself sick, only in this case it can give you the urge to shit.

Like a lot of sensitive men, I find it hard to piss in a urinal if anyone else is there; I put it down to long term insecurity in my case, too many rejections from women have left me feeling inadequate. In fact the number of hard knocks I've suffered at the hands of the 'unfairer sex' has left me with 'prostatodynia/prostatitis', and a dose of VD, cured now thankfully. (?)

My urinary flow became a trickle, with a burning sensation in the end of my knob, and with all the anxiety I've suffered, I think I forgot how to get started; standing there, pressing down from my stomach when really I need to exert internal pressure, 2 inches above my 'exhaust pipe'.

And thanks to the use of bee pollen pills and/or Saw Palmetto, (the latter are too expensive and not as effective for me) the trickle's turned back to a flow at times, and I don't have painful ejaculations when I wank , (what else can I do, go to bed wearing boxing gloves securely taped up?) Whoever would have made the connection between bee pollen and the prostate? It's all part of the holistic miracle isn't it? I wonder if any part of the human biology could be of use to any other animal species, or is it just one-way traffic from them to us?

....

'HOUSE TRAPPED IN THE SUN'.

I watched 'HOUSE TRAPPED IN THE SUN' last night, it was great fun, sitting crouched over my gas fire on 'economiser', to watch these ex pat' brits, a bunch of moaning gits, whinge and whine about how their foreign idylls had all gone horribly pear-shaped. Surely they weren't expecting sympathy from the likes of me, whose only hope of escape from England's (green with envy) and (un)pleasant land is a substantial win on the lottery?

The presenter was really fit, I kept trying to imagine her with her kit off, and nearly succeeded too; she looked like ultra high maintenance, the kind of woman I could never hope to aspire to, unless I won the European lottery too, (bitterly sarcastic laugh.)

Yes, eternally blue skies and views to die for is what this unfortunate bunch thought they were buying into; either in France or in Spain; now one of them is 'dying' from the stench and emotional pain, due to a sewage works materialising 100 yards away from her swimming pool. Her Mediterranean home is now literally worthless, except perhaps in its weight in shit.

I think hers was the most extreme case of continental 'egg on face', and they're all howling, 'Foul! Unfair play!' It's their own fault for thinking they could forsake old England and carry on as if they were still here, ignoring the natives, drinking imported chilled beer at their exclusive golf clubs; well the snubbed locals have had the last laugh in their cases, just like broken noses alter faces...take mine for instance.

....

I'M HORN CRAZY.

They're fucking crazy round here, and as 'redneck' as they come; they're too fat-arsed lazy to leave their vehicles when they want somebody to come to the door, so they beep their horns repeatedly; much to the consternation of me, myself, and I Try as I might, I can't mentally block it out. In the past I used to shout through my double-glazed window, 'Cut it out you shit-for-brains arseholes!', but I got warned off about that 'unacceptable level of anti social behaviour' by Pennine Housing 2000, PH2K for short; the association that charges far too much rent for a bungalow which could fit inside a family-sized tent; a small family that is, one adult and one child.
Rednecks with demonic powers, it really is uncanny; nine times out of ten if I open a window or a door, I'll be greeted by this infuriating, spiteful beeping noise, quite often when there's no vehicle in sight; it puts a blight on my day. It's a war of attrition between me and them; and sadly, I think they're winning. I can imagine their inverted ugly mugs evilly grinning as they slap a paw down on the blaring horn, as they race round this insignificant little estate from where I can't escape my fate; to be harassed and hounded by plebs till my dying day. Try as I may, I can't escape their tenacious grip, the drip, drip, drip of their redneck poison.
I really shouldn't let them get to me the way I do, just because I'm in the monkey's cage of this human zoo.

....

FURRY SHIT-HEADS.

Even the dogs round here are rednecks too, only good for turning pedigree pet food into smelly poo, and barking their fucking heads off; at times incessantly, or so it seems; an unwelcome accompaniment to a Beethoven symphony on Radio 3. Sometimes it's a toss-up as to whose causing the most annoyance, members of the radio audience coughing, or the miserable mutts ranting and raving out on the green or on the end of their chains, shit coming out of their arses, and shit-for-brains.
I haven't even touched on car alarms and burglar alarms going off at regular intervals, just to keep the pressure up. Why don't I just shut the fuck up moaning, or else do something about my situation you might well ask? Well, apart from writing down my grievances, there's not a lot I can do, I want to make money out of smug cunts like you buying my work; it paid off for 'Hank' Bukowski so why not for me? I don't want to shirk my social responsibility, but 'eight hours of nothingness' daily, (lowly paid employment of a menial nature, which is all I'm qualified for) to pay my rent is not what I was meant for; and my overall health problems won't allow it anymore.

'IS THAT ALL THERE IS' by Peggy Lee is one of my top tunes, its lyrics sum up the way I feel; I would steal some happiness given half a chance, even if it was only 'grab a granny' at the town hall tea dance....but no one's that unhappy...are they?

....

NUTTERS WITHOUT COATS.

I've seen a few reality TV programmes about nutters without coats. (Yes I know in polite society we don't use that derogatory term, we say 'people with mental health problems', but I'm not in polite society, I'm in my vituperative lair...so there.) I'm talking about our town and city centres at the weekends, when the loud and proud, in your face, animal night life comes out to play; it's getting more like Falaraki every Friday and Saturday night, gangs of plebs looking for a fight if things aren't going their way on the dance floor, and they're not going to score for a shag off some slag who's off her tits on tequila slammers, with her skirt up her arse and a see through top on.
It's our much-maligned cops who have to go wading in at chucking out time, risking life and limb to separate these nutters without coats from ripping each other's throats out.
I think up to about 25-years-old you don't feel the cold as much as you do after that; I know I was more foolhardy when I was young.
If I'd been able bodied enough to sign up to join the police force, I'd have strong reservations about this line of duty, unless I was issued with body armour, a stunner and a can of mace or pepper spray; I wouldn't risk getting my head kicked in by this form of human dross armed with anything less

....

FUCKING CUNTS.

Sounds fairly crude doesn't it, put like that? But when ladies have sexual intercourse, that's what they do, fuck with their cunts, unless they take it up their 'Gary Glitter', (that's 'shitter' to you and me); and anyway, fuck and cunt are two powerful old words, stretching back into antiquity. When that whining old pseudo punk, has been, Johnny Rotten said, 'You fucking cunts' on live: 'I'M A CELEBRITY, GET ME OUT OF HERE!' a few weeks back, it caused a ripple of disapproval through the nation, 91 complaints to

OFCOM secured a full apology from ITV. But across the water in the USA, when Janet Jackson's right tit popped out on live TV, a 'wardrobe malfunction', it caused a furore; 250,000 e-mails of complaint and a multi billion dollar law suit issued for a 'faint' a woman suffered after seeing this exposed mammary gland. I saw a photo of it in THE DAILY STAR, and I have to say it didn't inspire me to get my knob out and wank it; it looked to me like her elbow was sticking out from her chest, surrounded by black PVC. Bugger me, what is the world coming to when people swoon at the sight of a pair of mooning cheeks? If it's a wench who's doing it I'd be in there like a shot, covering her bum with my willy's snot.

(Update: The taboo over the 'c' word is wobbling a bit now, thanks to Channel 4's liberal use of it in 'comedy prog's'; and I've heard schoolgirls call each other it, and the loathsome Lea Walker used it last night on 'BIG BROTHER', when she was forced to 'walk' out to meet the baying mob after being evicted. And earlier this year [2006], Germain Greer was seen on BBC2, writing this powerful and evocative word 'CUNT', large upon on a wall in red paint; wanting us all to celebrate its fecundity. 'Cund' sounds a bit like 'cunt' doesn't it? 8/7/06.)

....

PLACE YOUR FAITH IN YOURSELF.

I almost feel sorry for those who are bathed in love, for when that love has gone for whatever reason, they have to fall back on themselves and make that long uphill climb to recovery, and not everyone makes it.

The less you are loved, the more you can learn to love yourself, or at least learn self respect; and there are plenty of those who don't achieve that either.

I've always had disability and life's always been a struggle for me, I tried putting my faith in The Lord, but whatever agency that is, it just laughed and said, 'You're on your own son, it'll make a man of you', and do you know, it's true!

I tried placing my faith in The Devil, offering to sell my soul for sex, fortune and fame, but whatever agency that is, it made no reply...and no deal either; I hope it doesn't come to collect me on my dying day, I'll feel really cheated if it does.

I was inspired to write this piece after walking nearly a mile home on a bitterly cold winter's night, totally alone in the world; but at least I had a home to come home to, with light and heat and something to drink and eat if I wanted it; a rough sleeper might well have died in a bus shelter or shop doorway.

Now I regard being loved by others very warily, the thought of deep commitment bores me, I want to be a user and exact my revenge on the female sex, in the nicest possible way of course. All you enigma-loving, literary ladies out there will have to make up your own minds whether I'm genuine or not in my misogynistic sentiments; so come on...MAKE MY DAY!!!

(I've entered this one into The Bridport Arts Centre Poetry Comp', if it doesn't win or get placed, there just ain't no justice for me in this world, but I knew that already didn't I?)

The dirty rotten fuckers couldn't spot poetic genius when it was glaringly staring them in the face; I dare say it will be the same this year too, the poo-heads! Maybe if I hadn't used the line: 'Fuck off you fucking nutter' in my entry for 2006, I might have stood a chance? But apart from the money and a bit of exposure, I'm not prepared to dance to their particular tune. 8/7/06)

....

BOW DOWN TO ME.

Bow down to me for I am the word, the law-giver and maker of the turd. I am the most heinous cabal of all, perhaps second only in power to the elected leaders of this land, and who knows, maybe I pull their strings as well? How did it ever come to pass that that which Charles Dickens called an ass can destroy people's lives if they lose at court? Why is it so expensive to get involved with the legal profession? And where do all the billions go that they cream off annually? Offshore tax havens perhaps? Mansions? Yachts? Fast cars? Priceless paintings? Issuing writs against mouthy gits like me?

In 'primitive society', the village elders meet to sort out policy beneath a tree, and rankling matters get talked through; sometimes the speaker can only speak when holding the tribal totem, but that's about it. None of this dressing up in wigs and gowns, like outdated clowns, and every minute of their time costing you an arm and a leg; (if you were wanting to sell either of these limbs on the Internet for transplant purposes that is.) Law fees should be pegged to 'real world' values, and be available to all; not just the privileged few. The only time it's free at source is when you're up on a charge. And then if you feel like telling the judge to FUCK OFF!, he'll give you more time freely, while looking down on you with a steely glare; but you're a hardened crim' so you just don't care.

I HAD A SHAG IN MY SLEEP LAST NIGHT. (T he title redolent(?) of The Electric Prunes: 'I HAD TOO MUCH TO DREAM LAST NIGHT'.)

Most of the wet dreams I have aren't very good, I either go off too soon or don't go off at all; waking up breathing heavily, hardly remembering what the theme was about and relieved that I wasn't going to have to wipe spunk off my belly on to the top sheet. But last night, BINGO! It was a proper fuck, albeit Far too short. She had black hair and a nearly clean shaven fanny, I don't know if it would be called a Brazilian or a Californian shave down; I prefer hairy mot's myself, the hairier the better.
Anyway, she was naked on the bed, oddly enough there was a naked man next to her but she was inviting me, and without any qualms I climbed over him and went straight into her primed vagina; like I said, it didn't last very long and I came like a rocket, exclaiming, 'No, no! You're going to be pregnant after this.' I woke up shortly afterwards and there was a big wet patch on my pyjama bottoms. I had to take them off because I didn't want to lie in a cold patch of congealed come. Now why can't I get this in real life? Some black - haired beauty who'll lay my soul to waste? As long as she'd sit on my face I wouldn't care, and let me tit fuck her now and then; she could lick the tip of my cock at the same time. (Update, I haven't felt the need to wear pyjamas since I left the outskirts of Todmorden, nearly 2 years ago; there was a kind of cold there that seeped into your very soul…if you had one…which most of the locals seemed to lack. 10/7/06.)

....

100 YEARS OF JUST ME & MY TV.

When you haven't been out socially for what seems like a hundred years, especially with a member of the opposite sex if that's your natural preference; and in my case I haven't had a date in the proper sense of the word since I was born, (surely I exaggerate? The last time I had a meal with a woman was in 2002, and there was one long hell of a gap before that.). Certain aspects of human behaviour tend to take on a strange hue , like kissing and dancing for instance.
Kissing's okay to do in the dark, in bed with someone you want to be with (as long as their breath doesn't smell), but to see other people do it…on TV, makes my flesh crawl; I have to steel myself to watch what looks like vampirism taking place; all that lips on lips sucking going on. Some years ago, when I said I hated lipstick to an awful woman I knew, she thought I was a

homosexual; my preference is for perfume or scent, either behind the ears or on the neck, or both.

I like to see women dance, the more sensually the better, dirty dancing. When couples do it I suppose it's part of the mating ritual, guys in a close together clinch with their girls with hard-on's; (I know that happened to me once, twenty-odd years ago, I was smooching with my ex best mate's wife in a club and I had a full stalk on; luckily we were both a bit pissed at the time because she was quite reserved about that sort of thing; she'd literally sleep with me but I wasn't supposed to grope her, who can fathom the female mind?), which again I suppose is okay as long as you don't prematurely ejaculate.

Today is my 57th birthday, no cards, no 'pressies', no one calling just to say 'I love you'. I have a small font of hope which does spring eternal, I think it's mixed with the elixir of life, though there are times when both miraculous substances seem to dry up, and I'm in danger of being dashed to pieces on barren rocks of hopelessness and despair; I have a dream and a long term plan and a chin like Desperate Dan. I could have a good life in Thailand if I could afford to live there, I wouldn't go short of female attention, and not necessarily in an exploitative way either. But what eats at the very core of my being is to never have had what so many people born here take for granted, a loving and productive relationship with an 'English Rose'.

I can only stand on the outside looking in at life through my TV screen. When I'm out it's the same, I'm mesmerised by really shaggable-looking women, but I'm now so conditioned to my unattractiveness that I can't look at them directly; (it was the same when I was 16, 17, 18, 19, & 20, etc), and what would I have to offer them anyway? Not even a successful writing career to back me up. The corrosive effect of all this accumulated stress and pressure has meant that I just hold on to my nerves by the skin of my teeth, and the slightest thing can send me off on a downward spiral of alarm and distress. The last nine years of my tortured (and I don't use that word lightly) life existing in the backward-looking town of Todmorden, ('A Town Called Malice' or 'The Church Of The Poisoned Minds'), hasn't done me any good at all. I wish I knew what really made these people tick, but then again I don't; naked greed and one-upmanship would be a good bet.

I just want to escape from the chilling stranglehold this volatile atmosphere's got me caught up in.

....

PEOPLE WITH VULNERABLE FACES.

There aren't many places for people with vulnerable faces to fit in easily. I don't want to be seen out with someone as crucially disadvantaged as me, it's top totty or nowt; the kind of girls whose tits you want to suck, whose clits you want to fuck and whose arseholes you want to stick your tongue in; (you've heard the expression, 'I'd have used her shit for toothpaste' haven't you?) Ugly man, 'should wear a bag over his head', Fred Elliot is the most extreme case of women looking with their ears I can think of; it's queer how he attracts female attention. I say it's queer how Fred Eliot attracts female attention! (The amorous, skin-headed butcher always proposes twice before he gives up. [Surely, none of my potential readers won't know who Fred Elliot is? I'm not aiming at T.S. Elliot readers here, I'm sure Fred's no relation to T.S. Elliot.])

....

ME NERVES ARE CRAWLIN', WHAT AMMA GONNA DO?

Do you ever get the feeling that someone out there is out to get you for no valid reason other than their rabid rat's eyes in their soulless rat's heads have seen you and you look like a likely victim to them? So you become afraid to go out after dark in case one or more of these creatures pounce. And what you don't know is they're gnawing through your telephone cable and as soon as they're able they're going to hurl themselves at your windows and come crashing in, wielding pick-axe handles and evil grins; they're not necessarily going to kill you, just destroy you internally and all you possess, leaving your precious CD collection in an awful mess.

....

NUTTERS WITH KNIVES AND ENOUGH BAD ATTITUDE TO USE THEM. (This hopefully will be the final piece in my seventh and definitely last collection.)

There was an all too familiarly horrible story on a local news bulletin the other night. A dirty little psycho had threatened revenge against his ex girlfriend for helping to get him banged-up for armed robbery; I think he only did a short stretch. When he got out he contacted this gullible female, (she was 22 years old), and persuaded her to meet him out in the open somewhere secluded; he enlisted his twin brother and his girlfriend to make sure his intended victim couldn't escape.

Obviously, I don't know if he ever intended to talk with her, but this dirty little posycho ended up stabbing her 18 times, so now it's back inside the slammer again, this time for murder; just one more to add to the growing ranks of thoroughly evil human rats festering away in our prisons. I saw his mug shot on the news as well, if I had to share a cell with him I'd strongly consider topping myself, or goad him into doing it for me. Because he's a killer now with a reputation to uphold and deserving of 'respect' according to the criminal's code; maybe he should be put in with Ian Huntley, Britain's most hated child murderer; he killed girls too, and they could brag together about their exploits, or vie for who gets possession of the top bunk.

The criminal code I'd subscribe to is Huntley being found hanged in his cell, the victim of an apparent suicide. Mind you, if you keep threatening him that's what's going to happen, you might eventually force his hand, though he's such a cowardly piece of shit I doubt it.

....

I HATE MY FACE. (Positively the very last entry in my Seventh Heaven Connection collection.)

I hate my face, it's a disgrace as far as faces go, and now that my firm jaw line's been replaced by something that looks uncomfortably like a double chin, I wouldn't mind kicking it in.

It's no wonder women don't take pity on me in my lonely state, I'd hate to be seen out in company with a mug like mine, even a skinful of wine wouldn't make it anymore endearing than a bulldog chewing a wasp.

Which brings me to the horror of relationships, if a certain young lady fell under my charms I'd be so scared of losing her I'd never let her out of my very limited sight or arms, which could make mobility rather awkward, two steps back and one step forward.

So it's the reclusive life for me, quite rightly, ugly people should neither be seen or heard; I suppose it's God's sense of the absurd that's responsible for our harrowing existence, I've reached the point of no resistance, with little else to say; what's that line from Otis Redding's 'DOCK OF THE BAY'? 'Looks like nothin's gonna come my way'? I suppose I could sit on a bench on the canal bank humming this, my favourite blues song, (apart from 'BORN UNDER A BAD SIGN'), wondering whether or not to throw myself in? Fuck that, I can't even swim and there's rats that piss in the water, giving you that awful, potentially fatal disease whose name I can't even spell.

....

AN ENVIRONMENT OF MISFORTUNE. (Defo' the last one; a bit like Defoe on his desert island hideaway after he slaughtered his last sheep....pure literary licence there, I assure you.)

Earlier this year I filled in a questionnaire on a full page in a Sunday tabloid newspaper for The International Parapsychology Centre in the Netherlands. They're apparently carrying out a major research programme into the psychology of winning big monetary prizes; seemingly it's not all down to luck. I got a detailed response back last Saturday, it all seems to be a coded request for money, (as in 'SEND US SOME!') off those of us who're either gullible or can easily afford to part with £32+£3 P&P; (normal price £89), for an even more detailed response from their internationally renowned psychic, Ezmeralda.
For my 32 quid, she'll issue me with a chart of favourable and unfavourable dates to try and win big bucks, plus my golden numbers and contact numbers, plus two séances just for me to increase my 'luckability'; (I just made up a new word inspired by 'fuckability') factor, and also include a personal talisman. Well I'm not gullible enough, or well-heeled enough to send her 35 quid. What I gleaned from reading the IPPC's report is that I was born (howling with protest no doubt) on a Wednesday, and my golden number is 9, a number I've never felt particularly drawn to, always preferring 3,5,7,or 11; and most crucially of all, based on my responses to the questions asked by them, I'm living in an 'environment of misfortune'.
Well I already knew that!!! Especially since I've just endured a spate of unwelcome attention from teenage yobs on the estate, initially pelting my windows with snow and ice balls. And after I'd loudly protested in the most basic English I could muster, coming back at night and banging loudly on my windows...very unnerving.
I can tell you what terror feels like to me, it feels like I've been given an electric shock mingled with debilitating fear; I start to shake and tremble and my mouth goes dry, making me about as effective in dealing with these vicious morons as the proverbial limp rag. Usually, by the time I've mastered this overpowering sense of fear and revulsion, they've fucked off, making the bucket of cold water I keep lined up to throw over them redundant.
Esmeralda did say I was going to enjoy a 'hot period between late Aril and late July, my hottest day being May 5th at 9pm. Well I expect to be in Thailand

on that date, and short of being up to my nuts in guts with a bar girl, (hopefully not a 'lady boy'), I can't think what she means. At least she's not forecasting imminent doom and advising me not to travel...

....

KILL CRAZY AFTER ALL THESE YEARS.

Thou shalt not kill...for the thrill of it, even if you feel sorely, severely provoked; choked up with impotent rage. 'Vengeance shall be mine sayeth the Lord' should be my motto, I have so much pay back time due to me. First against God Almighty himself and his heavenly crew. Of course the whole concept of 'God' is a farce, just so much evil wind blown out of the human arse. Did this omnipotent being wait nearly 4 billion years, ever since the world began, to give birth to his most diabolical creation, man? And if he did, would 'he' be dumb enough to send his only begotten son down here, knowing what the likely outcome would be?
He abuses me, he makes me lie down with a nest of vipers, having first removed my eyes; it's an S & M relationship between the arbiter of my fate and me. But even the worm turns so they say, a sight I've yet to see. Although I long to kill my tormentors, a cowardly and peevish lot, so much snot on the evolutionary scale; I wouldn't want to spend time in an actual gaol where the shit-stabbing arse bandits prevail. And I don't want to end up becoming some 'daddy's' rather butch-looking bitch.
If only I could find a witch who could give me a hellish-vermin proof talisman to ward of these tics, I'd spend the rest of my time fending off her black magic tricks for lack of payment.

....

I'VE THE MIND OF A 27-YEAR-OLD TRAPPED INSIDE THE BODY OF A MUCH MALIGNED AND BELEAGURED 57-YEAR-OLD MAN.
(Hounded unto death perhaps.)

'If you want my body and you think I'm sexy, c'mon sugar let me know'? No? I thought so, it's just my crippled libido won't let go, insisting on equal opportunities for the job; only prob' is, my face isn't qualified and I don't possess the two years required experience of regular sex. My ego's a lot like that too, pushing and thrusting, trying to break on through, especially when

I'm having mock sex with my semi clenched fingers and the palm of my hand…it takes me to the promised land for one.

And this writing too, I want to quit, I want to stop, but my ego keeps telling me I'm the cream of the crop. I should have my own knocking shop so I could knock copies of my work out as soon as I've penned them, on my trusty portable photocopier. Of course my ego's not got much else to focus on, what do you do when all your options are long gone, with only a win on the lottery to pin your hopes of escape on? Someone like me deserves to scoop a big pot, think of all the good I could do in the animal world if I had a few mill' to splash out? I could buy a chunk of rain forest and erect electric fencing to keep humans out and the animals in.

(In my original hand written version of this piece, I've written 'finish off on disc'; but I can't think of anything else to add, except perhaps that I don't particularly like animals, they're too weird-looking for me; take elephants for instance. But I hate cruelty on the scale that bloodthirsty humans practice it, and I don't see why everything else should be destroyed for human vanity.1/11/04.)

....

THE LONGER I REMAIN ALIVE THE MORE I CAN ACHIEVE.
(The teachings of 'Are Lah'. D'you gerrit? 'Are Lah'? 'Allah'? 'Our Lad'?!)

If you can stay alive no matter how much life will, all too willingly, throw at you, (and believe me I've had some really blood-soaked, soggy, newspaper wrapped parcels of filth shoved into my face), and still retain the same level of sanity you had as an innocent baby, you just might live to an overripe old age. Take me, I'm 57 now and quite often bowed by adversity, but never completely broken; I'm sometimes cowed in my chosen field, ('You cannot be serious!') by truly great writers like Gerald Kersh, a forgotten genius, (he's only been dead a few decades), in the helter-skelter rat race of the literary world.

The flags should be unfurled in his honour, he should be England's number one literary sun; we're all duffers compared to him, (well I feel I am anyway.) If you don't believe me, get hold of copies of 'THE ANGEL AND THE CUCKOO' and 'THE SONG OF THE FLEA'; how does one man acquire so much knowledge of human nature, good and bad, and still find time to write not one, but several masterpieces? My work is faeces compared to his. Now, am I saying that because I can't find a publisher worth a wank?

51

I'm reaching out to America now in a last desperate bid, BLACK SPARROW BOOKS might pay me a few quid for my jottings.

(Oh no they won't. The guy who owned and ran Bukowski's cash cow has retired, and BSB has been sold off. My bid to crack the American market fell on stony ground. The pain of failing is truly excruciating, it cuts like a knife into your psyche.)

....

LIVING IN FEAR OF DREAD. (And I'm not talking Judge Dredd here.)

I have a fear born out of revulsion, of brute ignorant stupidity. The more ignorant the brute, the more likely it is to resort to violence as a means of gaining 'respect' among its peers; it's a throwback to when we were chimpanzee-type animals. Every species has this trait of the male needing to prove itself, and when it cant, or it gets too old, it's either banished from the group or else gets killed off.
In humans it's usually the pleb' male who's most to be feared, because it lacks the basic intelligence to behave in anything other than a primitive way; it can't use its intellect to reason things through because it DOESN'T HAVE ANY! What it does know, and uses to full advantage, is that nice, civilised people are, in the main, terrified by violence; I know I am. If we didn't have the police to act as a barrier between them and us, we'd have a state of absolute terror, with mobs of low IQ, low achiever-type yobs using physical force to take whatever they wanted, from your home to your family.
I'm in the 'getting too old for this crap' category, my nerves and 'bottle' goes when any of these sub humans draws near and starts jeering at me. Short of becoming the proud owner of an AK47, I'm going to have to move 15 storeys up nearer to heaven. (Update, I now call this type of human madness [after being informed of the latest atrocities in Iraq], 'Barbaric Nihilism' or 'Savage Anarchy' The brute element in 'man' could destroy the whole world; a bit like the London fire-storm of December 29th, 1940, wiping out a square mile of English history. 10/7/06.)

(Well I've moved to the comparative safety of Halifax, not 15 storeys up as I envisaged, but one floor below HELL in the form of a 'theatre dance school'! How about that for bad luck dogging your trail? And on top of that, both tape decks on a cheap hi fi system I bought recently, have become unusable because tapes got stuck in them and I had to yank them out to free them, and

I never bothered to send the guarantee off within the 30-day period specified from the purchase date; what am I going to do? Boo Hoo!!!)

....

OPPORTUNITIES THAT SHOULD ARISE BUT DON'T.

You see someone who you could go for in a big way, but too much social decay has eroded that vital part of your brain which should enjoy the mating game; very ineffective eyesight doesn't help my cause along either.

I saw a vision of loveliness in a poppy-red dress and long dark hair, with a quiet air of mystery about her; ideally we should have walked off into the night together and consummated our newfound mutual adoration by dawn's early light. But she went off to an unknown destination and I went to the pub and sat with a bunch of boring old women, feeling too despondent even to buy a drink.

I did find out her name and the sad fact that she's married, but there might be problems there; her name is very romantic. I've taught myself not to care, if opportunities for self-improvement or advancement aren't there, not to give a damn. But even though I never spoke to her, I did have pangs of regret as I lay in my lonely bed last night.

I wonder if she thought anything of me after hearing me read? And will I see her again at the next writing and poetry evening in one month's time? I'll have put her on the back burner by then, too busy struggling for survival as just one more of today's marginalized men in Britain's crap society.

(Just to put you avid followers of my misfortunes out of your torments of wondering, 'Did he finally find a bit of romance?' The answer is no I fucking didn't get a fuck out of that particular situation; I've never seen that enigmatic creature again, she's probably into S&M, enjoying being tied up with strings of uncooked sausages, to be ripped off her and devoured by a slavering Rottweiler dog, and what happens after that the Devil only knows.)

....

AN EPIC PRO'S POEM. ('E'pic up pro's whenever e' can, E'm that kind of man.') (I think that's the shortest thing I've ever created, I hope you get it, it's quite funny if you do. Not that I've ever been with a 'working girl' in this country; street tarts have got such a bad reputation, and anything above that basic level is out of my price range. I'd love to be able to afford to pay an escort to be with me on Christmas Day if I have to be stuck here on my own; but this year I'm going away; the amount I'm paying for my holiday would probably cover a hooker's costs for a few hours if I was staying here, well there's no fucking fear of that! 460 quid just to shag some twat for a couple of times and then be on my own again? THE PAIN!)

....

THE AFTERNOON PLAY.

Me and the Radio 4 afternoon play, go back a long, long way. I first started seriously listening to the then Home Service, when I was 13 or 14; I loved nothing more than secreting myself away with the Saturday afternoon play. My mother would sometimes come up to my room to try and roust me out, saying Saturday afternoons were all about going to a football match, but to me that wasn't a patch on listening to the afternoon play.
The one time I did go to Main Road to 'see' Manchester City play, was on a Boxing Day when I was about 17; I was freezing cold, bored stiff, and on the way out I got waylaid by a posse of blokes lecturing me about the evils of long hair, I thought they were going to tear it out at the roots; my mates had to usher me away...I should have written a play about it.
It does irk me, the fact that I can't write plays, (or novels come to that). I sit here for days contemplating my awful fate, hating everything and everyone around me, only feeling safe in the dead of night; my nerves are so bad my stomach turns to shite at the slightest bump or bang. The play today was a pile of Scottish crap, some pap about Glasgow bints posing as artist's models.

(Yes, you get a whole host of oral entertainment on Radio 4, and to a lot lesser extent on Radio 3, plays galore; and if you like to listen to 'critics' rambling on, you can do. Not that they're just critics anymore, everything has to be pulled apart and gnawed at, quite possibly even destroyed; I call them THE VITRIOLICS, and they wield too much power. If they ever savaged anything of mine I'd have them kneecapped and acid thrown in their faces; I know just the crew to do it, naming no names, but one of their surnames rhymes with speed. (Which is how he leaves the scene of one of his maulings, RAPIDO TORPEDO!)

....

PIRACY ON THE HIGH C's
(SCRAPING THE BOTTOM OF THE BARREL FOR APPLES.)

What became of the broken hearted whose love departed after he farted and stank the house out, making such a stench she just couldn't forgive, let alone live with. After she left he ate and drank himself to death, his very last breath came out in a long belching croak, giving off a stink like rotting fish and industrial strength ammonia. His face looked like the Satanic depiction of the god Saturn by Goya. They decided to turn his house into a mausoleum and filled it with concrete to kill the smell of his feet.

JC was an ET, AE was the father of the AB. Do you ever get the impression that the 'civilised world' is rapidly heading towards MELTDOWN? That if the food supply ever dried up, we'd really see anarchy in the UK? The whole of middle England swept away in a tide of resentful plebeian backlash, violent activity; all that 'Mickey Mouse' house price rise money not worth the paper it's printed on, and all that pretentious swagger gone for good? It should happen here, it should, it should! I know I sometimes fantasise about the sound of machine gun fire when I see footage of muslims praying to their chosen god in mosques in England's green and pleasant land; if we could clean up after foot and mouth disease, I'm certain we could do the same after we'd dealt with these wasp-like, alien fanatics. (My god! [who I don't believe in], have I just incriminated myself for advocating ethnic cleansing at some unspecified time in the future? I hope I won't be here to see it, I hope I'll be sunning myself in Thailand or burnt to ashes in a crematorium; I hate violence.)

That outburst probably surpasses my right to 'free speech'; muslims can preach religious hatred but not us. Being white has almost become a dirty word in middle England, all I can say is, 'Imagine a world order under Bin Laden and The Taliban? No man, woman or child would be safe from the random wrath of these totalitarian monsters.'

I've often suspected that the bulk of humanity has inane (no I don't mean 'innate') bad taste; how else could someone like Will Young be riding on the crest of popularity, and even receiving awards for his 'singing'? If I didn't know he was 'gay', would I suspect him anyway after hearing his awful castrato vibrato warblings? But after the success of the totally bizarre Micheal Jackson, I suppose there aren't any depths the general public won't sink to when it comes to bad taste.

Yes, Jesus was an extra terrestrial, and Albert Einstein was the father of the atom bomb, making him an anti Christ. And why does humanity need to place its bloody faith in invisible beings? Is it so it can forgive itself for the evil that mainly men do? It's not only the planet that's heating up, the levels of hatred are reaching boiling point too; could this world ever become as hot and barren as the planet Venus? All life wiped out by our rash acts? Maybe that's it, 'Whom God will destroy he'll first make mad', but he's going to destroy everything else in doing so; just when he had the balance right on this god-forsaken blue planet as well....

(I do apologise for using the word 'he' when it comes to talking about this supposed super deity. Quite probably the universe is merely a conglomeration of totally inhospitable and chaotic masses. Ours is the only world we can safely live on, and we're busily turning it into a wasteland to satisfy our short-term greed; not that I'm any less greedy than the next human, I just like to think I might do some good in the world if I could ever get my hands on a substantial stash of cash; like tomorrow night's tenth lotto free birthday draw for £10 million.)

....

I WANNABE A SPERM BANKER.

I read today that there's a sperm donation shortage on the way, well I've been tossing mine away free for years and years; under the sad impression that no one wanted it; treating it as the necessary evil conclusion to a physically and mentally hygienic 'fifty off the wrist' wanking session. Which is preferable to seeking out some dodgy street tart to give you a short, sharp knee trembler for twenty quid or more, down a back alley, wondering whether her pimp's going to come along and roll you, right when you're on the vinegar strokes with your pants down.

You can pay a lot more, I rang an escort agency the other day, it worked out at £200 for 2 hours; I didn't ask if that included 'golden showers'? My penis had shrivelled up too much for me to care.

....

TATTERED DEMALION STALLION, or RAGGED-ARSED STUD.

Just imagine if my sperm was acceptable, I could be making deposits every week, it would speak volumes for my manly pride. And if the recipients wanted to know my pedigree, they could be told, 'It's Phil Fletcher's, the poet, don't you know.' ('I don't know him, what's he wrote?'). 'He's tall and still has most of his own teeth, it's our belief that if you're looking for a donor of jutting chin and noble brow, you'd best accept this spunk right now seeing as there's a shortage, and he really wants to be a dad. He'll be thrilled if, in 18-years time, some strapping lad comes banging on his door, demanding to know if the ugly fucker who's opened it is the one responsible for all the jibes and taunts he's had to endure. Say no more.'

....

THE BURNLEY BLUES BOAT CRUISE.

With a face like mine I was born to sing the blues, so as part of Burnley's Easter Blues Festival, I took a ride on a blues boat cruise. I don't live in Burnley, and one of the first things that struck me was how well complemented the town shopping centre is; no credit to the BNP I would have thought.

I'd bought my ticket in advance over the phone, paying a pound extra for the privilege. 'BLUE C' was the outfit I'd paid to see, 'C' as in vitamin, not the tropical azure that lures us off to faraway places, even if we can't swim and don't like the sea anyway, you never know what you might tread on.

After asking a lot of people for directions I finally found the Burnley Mechanics Institute, though I didn't spot anyone in blue overalls leaning against a wall drinking a mug of tea. My venue was further up the road from it, I arrived on board the Marton Emperor a few minutes before the regally named barge was due to set off at 2pm; I grabbed a seat at the back, right next to where the cold draught blew in from the open entrance. There was a compact bar behind me which I ignored, I've a dread of walking round with a full bladder and seemingly nowhere to empty it; and I can't go either if I feel stressed out, it's a form of involuntary water retention that I always get in public loos or on aeroplanes, especially if there's a queue waiting impatiently outside.

I couldn't really see Blue C, they were too far up the boat for me and the lighting was rather dim; but they sounded good, her on electric bass and slide guitar, and him on acoustic guitar and 'harp'. I could relate to every miserable song they sang, and their depressive ambience blended in well with the over-abundant debris floating past us on the Burnley Cut. I could put up with that, but what got to me was these two guys behind me propping up the bar, they didn't stop 'jarring' from 2pm till 3, one of them bragging he'd spent 130 quid over the festival weekend, mostly on booze.

During my 3 hours in Burnley I didn't spend a penny, I should have turned round and told him and his mate to shut the fuck up, that I'd paid £6 to enjoy this 60 minute trip; and possibly throw in a quip that a fool and his money are easily parted. But that might have started a rumble, with me ending up in the murky four-or-five foot deeps of the mucky canal, thenceforth to sleep with the barely alive fishes in the putrid mud on the bottom. I was determined to immortalise these two in infamy in my rise to fame; they probably don't read poetry anyway, being too busy drinking their money away and marring people's holiday.

(And to round off what should have been a pleasant Sunday afternoon's diversion, when I got off the bus and began walking up the steep incline to my 'bungalow', I got waylaid by this shagnasty teenager as I was coming out from under a bridge; this creature lobbed an insult at me in a guttural voice, so I hurled a few back. He didn't like this and began throwing stones of increasing size at my retreating back; I'm only glad he was a lousy shot, or else I would have arrived home dripping blood from a freshly acquired wound to my face or head.)

···

YOU WOULDN'T WANT TO BE FEELING BORBORYGMIC IN AN INTIMATE SITUATION, LIKE A '69ER' FOR INSTANCE; IT WOULD BE EQUIVALENT TO A FARTING FANNY.

Sex in the head can be a lot more exciting than sex in the bed. With sex in the head you retain control, if you want it earthy and raw, you can do, with no fear of recriminations; it's more hygienic too. Yes, it's dirty and you know you want it, but you don't want to pay for it, and you don't want to join a group of kinky swingers either; you want it one on one with a woman of your choice. Two consenting heterosexual adults fornicating freely.

Of course, sex in the head, (and in the hand) might be the best I'm going to get in this septic Isle of corpulent greed and self-interest. My idea of a 'last tango' went out of style some years ago, being replaced with 'girl power' and the new ladette culture. I think women expect their sex beasts to be a bit younger than me, who might have a seizure, or just seize up if I found myself in a three-in-a-bed sex romp with two seventeen-year-old nymphomaniacs; (I know I said I wanted 'one on one' but my imagination got carried away with itself). What a way to go tho', 'ay? Two lovely young, firm limbed, flat bellied, full breasts and buttocks, fun loving girls, letting you do whatever you want with them again and again...in your fevered brain!!!

···

IT'S INCROYABLE.

(That's just a fancy word for 'incredible', I've picked it from a book by Gerald Kersh, along with 'borborygmic'.)

I heard a piece of music by Mahler this afternoon, I think it was from his 4th symphony but I can't be certain. It's climactic moments were like having your emotions dragged over barbed wire and jagged broken pieces of glass; it was so full of sadness and despair. If I was going to kill myself because I couldn't stand anymore of the mindless evil I'm constantly subjected to, I'd have this on my CD player before I kicked the bucket from under me at the heart-rending climax. Bob Dylan wrote a song many moons ago called, 'I AM A MAN OF CONSTANT SORROW' which I only ever heard by Rod Stewart when he was still vaguely credible, 30-odd years ago; now he sounds like Macy Grey and looks like Fagin, with his eagle beak and dyed blonde hair.
Of course he'd sue the arse off me if he ever read this put down of his unjustified career. Well, Rod my dear, sue me and be damned to Hell, along with your bimbos, you hook-beaked joke of a man. Now where was I? Oh yes, a man of constant sorrow? Well I'm a man under constant distress, making my life a much bigger mess than it needs to be. It's incredible how a peace-loving man like me can have so many enemies. Admittedly, a lot of them aren't very bright, but there's something out there mind-stalking me, with a 'soul' as black as the blackest night, and as heavy and dense as a black hole. I believe this thing wants me destroyed; it's done its worst to psychically kill me.
But if you tried to find out the reason why, you couldn't; I know I can't. Anyone experiencing this level of mindless, moronic, motiveless, malicious malevolence, should read Guy de Maupassant's 'THE HORLA'; it put this feeling of being menaced into perspective for me, though I'm not recommending you carry out it's conclusion to the letter. It's better to circumnavigate this evil whenever you can by adhering to a plan of being pointlessly happy with simple things like music, a good book, small gains; I would have thrown in a good fuck but I can't get one of those, it's the mindless one's main weapon against me, forcing me to live a life of celibacy in the land of my birth.
My largely mirthless existence has ruined my health, I'm riddled with arthritis and severe neuralgia and pains in my head; in many respects I'd be better off dead, but I'm going on holiday instead. I hope the intense heat will defeat the ice-cold nature of my nadir, a queer I mistakenly let inside my defences many years ago when I was young and naïve.
(My third holiday in Thailand this year was my best ever, my move to Halifax should have taken all the pressure off me, but because of a cruel twist of fate it hasn't, I maybe moving soon but it could mean more upheaval. 6/11/04)

TRITURATION IN THE WIND.

Some events happen all too slowly, like winter turning into spring, and on the other hand other things just piss past, like my life rotating on its seven-day cycle faster than a Whirling Dervish on overdrive. I've said that the longer I live the more I can achieve; mentally this is true, but at my present rate of progress I might need to live till I'm 200 or more. At a socially and emotionally isolated 57, I reckon I'm on a par with your average spotty adolescent; I've yet to achieve adulthood in the relationship sense; if only my hips were those of a pneumatic youth.
My mind's as uncouth as that of a horny 18-year-old, and older women leave me cold. Any woman over 45 who hasn't looked after her skin and figure is an insult to her sex. England expects every man to do his duty as far as obese old bats are concerned, well I'll leave them to our new black brothers who seem to have blinkers on when it comes to these old ruins; they don't seem to mind being socially spurned; give me a vibrant young woman every time, even if I'm going to get my penis burned from doing it six times a night once I've got up to full steam. It's every old lecher's dream isn't it? 200quid for two hours with a tasty escort will be my only hope of SUCK SEX.

....

DEVIL DOLL.

You sent me a devil doll to show me you loved me; you stabbed a pin right through its heart. You couldn't stand me while we were together; you've chosen to hate me now that we're apart.

....

FUTURE WOIRLD TODAY, DEAD WORLD TOMORROW.

Faster, faster, burn out faster trying to obey your technological and profiteering master; you can, and will be replaced. 12 hundred million (and rising) Chinese can't be wrong.!!!!!!!!!!!!!!

....

COOKING HELL!

Now I'm a man who's quite partial to swearing, but watching Gordon Ramsey on so-called 'reality TV', really did my cooking head in. He's worse than Billy Connolly for using the 'f' word on screen, making it sound rather obscene. Oh cook it, who gives a flying cook anyway!?

....

DEATH'S HEAD INTERLOPER.
(More unnecessary pain and suffering.)

I feel the pressure from your rotting skull inside my head, you're an aspect or vestige of the undead, clinging round me like a killer vine strangling the life out of a healthy tree; you'll probably 'live' on long after me, cocooning my husk all empty and hollow.

....

ODE TO MIDSUMMER.

It's Midsummer's Eve and I've got the gas fire on, we've had a spot of warm weather but now it's gone; it's been a few days since the sun shone cleanly and clearly on my back door, and you have to be up early in the morning to catch it doing that, the devious two-faced twat.
If Vaughn Williams Lark tried ascending round here it would end up with a nasty rasping cough; someone's been burning rubber off in the copse over yonder, leaving me to ponder my future through a greasy-smelling purple haze, longer nights and shorter days.
Who says that selling your soul for a brief taste of happiness doesn't pay? I can't even give mine away. For a rollover jackpot win on the national lottery and the young woman of my schemes, I'd unwillingly roast for all eternity; though the prospect of having a red hot poker shoved up my arse and coming out through the top of my head, doesn't seem very nice, even though I'll be one of the undead. Unless, like Christopher Marlowe's Faust, I could try and wriggle out of payment on Satan's soul-collecting day by saying, 'The money's all gone and she wasn't worth it anyway. Can we re-negotiate mate? Can I be a successful writer instead and enjoy lots of passionate love affairs? Why are you pointing to the downward moving stairs that seem to be descending into a bottomless pit? OH SHIT!!!'

THERE'S FUCK-ALL ON TV.

We've had to suffer stinking golf, cricket, and lousy boring football, 24-7; and now two weeks of the stinkiest pile of poo of them all, and for me, the most inscrutable of all these tedious sports in its enormous popularity…tennis!!!! Vindictively I hope that all the morons who follow it avidly, end up with their necks in braces from all that head swivelling in pursuit of that little yellow ball, from one end of the court to the other.

I like watching women's athletics now they're all wearing skimpy bottoms and tops, it's really rather thrilling when they bend over and give you nearly a full view; not unlike ladies ice skating where, if they weren't wearing flimsy knickers,, you'd be able to see right up their fundaments…PHWOARRRRRRR!!!!!!!!!!!

Glimpsing a peek of arse cheek and white pants from beneath a short flimsy tennis skirt can be more erotic than full frontal nudity; because basically that purloined view isn't openly on offer to you. A few years ago it would have been taboo. Yesterday afternoon while watching women's athletics on TV, I had a mild case of apoplexy when this high jumper landed in front of me, arse over tip; she was only wearing a bikini bottom and skimpy top, I nearly lost control of some seminal fluid…ooohhh!

....

'I HAVEN'T SEEN OLD SHIT-FACE LATELY.'

If I wasn't here, the same light would shine through my window, and the same programmes would be shown on TV, If I wasn't here not many people would miss me.

....

And here's a little quote from 'PETER COOK REMEMBERED' by his loving wife, Lin Cook; that vital ingredient that I've never inspired and which, along with a marked absence of success in my literary endeavours, has nearly killed me on numerous occasions: 'He looked happier with her there, more content, as if the demons which had haunted him in earlier years had wandered away—never totally out of earshot, but no longer perched on his shoulder, poking sharp noses in his business.'

I wish I could say the same, but I get made tangibly aware that black-hearted, black-minded psychic stalkers are still trying to control me from a distance; it's called being under psychic attack. I wish I could afford to pay a top spiritualist or medium to pinpoint and identify this scum to me, though I have strong suspicions of who at least two of these ESP perverts are. Once properly identified, I could have these psychic interlopers bumped off by pouring petrol over them and throwing a lighted match on them; I wonder if I'd laugh as they ran off roped together, screaming and ablaze.

(I now have 3 girlfriends, 2 in Thailand and 1 here, none of them 'hands on' of course, tho' I'm hoping to alter this emotionally painful situation in time; [it's fairly hard on my long suffering penis as well]. Mind you, once my English girlfriend has read this, with whom I was wishing to have an 'early spring and late autumn' relationship with...but no doubt I won't; still, that still leaves my two Thai girlfriends, and if they ever find out about each other then no doubt I'll have none! And as for the one that got away unsullied by me, and who I still think about tenderly, aaahhh! (deep sigh.) 11/11/04.

....

I'M INTO MINIMALISM TO THE MAX.

Sometimes I get an almost uncontrollable urge to pare everything down to its/their bare essentials, even my hair; I don't want to cut it all off and go 'skinhead', but nearly there, and the amount of possessions I've got makes me nearly despair.
In this age of super technology that's moving way too fast for me to understand it, ('I-PODS'? I'm still getting to grips with pea pod unzipping), I prefer to look back through a tunnel vision view of my past; and I'm getting more and more selective all the time; pretty soon there'll only be a pinpoint of bright light seen through a purple haze. Between '67 and '73 was the right time to be young for me; hip and cool, wild and free, indulging in the roller coaster ride of LSD. My 'ugliness' didn't haunt and taunt me the way it does today in this avaricious and discriminating country of my birth; the latter of these two human failings more covertly these days; you can be had up in court if you're too blatant in your prejudices and dislikes, of which I myself have plenty.
I have a low tolerance of the facially challenged, (especially my own), and the elderly and old. Though having seen my 86-year old father recently after a 4-

year gap, dispelled the prejudice and dislike I'd built up against him...for a short period anyway.

....

IT'S THE ALL NEW MOONLIGHT SHOW.

It's the silvery blue hue of a two-thirds full new moon, above the little woods opposite the living room window of my miniscule 'council' home; this is where I am right now in the world; (present time.) I've got 'ORBITAL' repetitively droning on in the background on TV, 'live' from Glastonbury. From what I've just heard, they're right to be packing it in, their stuff sounded like a hackneyed din. Trying to see up Jo Whiley's short dress as she fronts the BBC's coverage of the annual young person's ego fest is more entertaining to me, she keeps crossing and uncrossing her shapely legs...!
There's not enough variety in the BBC's coverage of Glastonbury for me, too many guitar bands are so yesterday, like Paul MacCartney, and even Morrissey, (the fucking cynical wanker!!!) Imagine my delight when late last night the Salford 'punk' poet, John Cooper-Clarke turned up in the hospitality tent; all too briefly, and wearing shades; still sporting a head of frenzied-looking black hair, and not saying much to 'cheesy' Mark Radcliffe. There was no chance of seeing his set; it might have got in the way of some of the more mainstream stuff. I'd love to have seen his bluff, gruff performance, that staccato voice clubbing his audience into an admission that he's still the UK's best alternative poet, (apart from me); a counter balance to John Hegley, and an icon for me. (Unlike Felix Dennis, who's an over-indulged pile of boring shite; never trust an old hippy, they're the worst 'bread heads' on the planet!)

....

BILLY FURY'S COMET.

Last night the moon was as big as a dinner plate, I sat up late to watch a gratuitous pile of British rubbish, a film called: 'LIFE OF STUFF'; it was supposedly about Glasgow gangsters, it was more like a take on 'MACBETH', lots of blood and death.
I kept looking out of my living room window at the full moon as it descended to earth behind the woods opposite. It was so bright it was like watching a

comet coming down in slow motion, surrounded by an aura of hazy light. It reminded me of an old Billy Fury song, 'Last night was made for love but where were you?', and a particular line: 'Were you looking at that same old moon in some other fella's arms'? etc, it definitely was a lover's moon.

There was a young woman in the awful film called 'Janice', who had the look that has always attracted me; I call it the Irish look; jet black hair, regular features in a pale peach complexion, like a young Sandie Shaw. I could imagine me and her shagging each other senseless under such a moon, in a tropical paradise; my failing health permitting.

But of course, it's not to be, as usual I'm on my own unnaturally, and never able to break the shackles of poverty and social isolation that bind me, always there to remind me that here in England my life's a pile of unrelenting SHITE!

....

UNLEASH THE COLOURS.

You can't have real psychedelia without LSD; mescaline would be better for me, not that I ever want any of that 'Heaven and Hell' chemistry again, and The Doors of perception can stay closed to me for the rest of my natural; I'd swap all that quest for eternal knowledge for a full flavoured pint mug of tea and four slices of white bread and strawberry jam (only on two of them latterly, a double chin's not for me), for breakfast every morning. Since I issued my own health warning a year or so ago, I've included a bowl of high fibre cereal as well, eaten dry on a small plate.

In an ideal world I'd be taking in the big sky while I munched on my sultana bran, the jewel in the crown of creation on a sunny summer morning. But the view from my kitchen window is marred by a house of horror at the back of me; even its window frames look charred. And if I venture out into my back garden to scent the balmy air, the locals soon know I'm there, sending me scuttling back in, in disgust at the din they deliberately make from car alarms, electric hedge trimmers, and a minor earth quake caused by a revving motor bike engine. All in all, my life's worth fuck all round here, a daily ritual of fear and loathing, waiting for THE END to come.

(That was an obituary for/to my sojourn on the Ashenhurst estate, Todmorden, where I did a two-year stretch; but my whole 18 years in Calderdale have been like this. Wherever I've attempted to make my home there've been shag nasty worms eagerly waiting to crawl out of the woodwork to give me a hard time. Being severely visually handicapped hasn't helped me any, but the whole blight has taken on much darker proportions; fate looking for another martyr, as if I'm supposed to endure a lousy existence so posterity can benefit from my misfortunes; like it did with Vincent van Gogh; it'll serve posterity right if I never get discovered.)

....

IAMBIC PARAMETER.

Let this be the last piece I ever write, because writing without recognition or reward, is a depressing pile of shite; my arms and hands are getting too stiff to hold a pen and this pad for very long, I really want this piece to be my swan song. I've given my style of creative writing everything I've got, it's not my fault if fate has lost the plot when it comes to me finding fortune and fame…I apportion no blame to myself.
Listen to this for a definition of IAMBIC (IAMB), and then tell me if I'm the only one who can't make head or tail of what it's supposed to mean: 'A metrical foot of two syllables, a short one followed by a long one. 2/ A line of verse of such feet.' As for 'pentameter', it gets worse, you just don't want to go there…believe me, unless you've got an IQ of E=MC squared. Go on, I dare you, give me a rational explanation of this formalised crap, (preferably after a few drinks). And if you do I'll eat my own poo out of a dunce's cap, and believe me again, you wouldn't want to put your snooty nose anywhere near that either.
I've no intention of dying or fading away, each new day is a challenge to me on how to keep myself alive in this heaving sea of adversity. I'll batten down my hatch until it's time to catch a one-way flight to my earthly paradise in the sun…this job's done.

....

OVEN CHIPS, THE BEST THINGS TO COME ALONG SINCE SLICED BREAD.

Can anyone remember how long it used to take to peel the spuds and cut them up to make chips to throw into a pan of dubiously dated oil, bubbling and gurgling with animal fat from all the sausages you've fried in it? I can, it took ages, and quite often the oil would be overheated by the time the wet raw chips hit the pan, causing a Vesuveus-like eruption of greasy steam shooting up the wall; I wouldn't go back to those days for all the unbridled passionate sex I'm never going to get, not unless I pay for it anyway; which in theory wouldn't bother me if the sex industry wasn't so murky.

At least with oven chips and sliced bread you know what you're going to get…that's right, a chip butty; a lot less smutty than a lap dancing club. Just imagine a beautiful naked woman dancing provocatively in front of you and all you can do is shove a rolled up £20 note up her flue or tight little butt? When I was young I thought creatures of the opposite sex were exotic and full of mystery; now I know it's a cover for promiscuity if the right catalyst comes along. My chemical formula has been put together in the wrong way to make me a fanny magnet here in the UK.

··

A BOLD AND DARING PROPOSITION.

I put a bold and daring proposition to someone who'd gotten her hooks into me, initially she acquiesced, but then apparently had a better offer; I really should have guessed it would end this way, it always does. Just when I've gained some semblance of faith in the opposite sex, another one comes along and puts a hex on it; leaving my nemesis cackling with glee, and me at the nadir end of ennui.

I was going to dedicate this final collection to K., but she used and abused me like all the rest so she can fuck off.   Phil Fletcher. (The very last word.)

(I am back in love with her again even though she's not around right now, I hope we can have an 'early spring' and 'late autumn' relationship, preferably on foreign shores, before she goes her inevitable way and I go mine; and where I'm thinking of, there'll always be more pebbles on the beach.)

··

UNREALISTIC EXPECTATIONS FROM A SHAG.

By the time she's juiced up and ready to go, you could have already 'come and gone' as it were. She's ready to let you put it in for the first time, but it's been primed and ready to blow for the last half hour's foreplay, so when she moans, 'Is that it?' as you lie there limply with your face in her tits, you bite her nipples playfully. If she's not the understanding kind who knows it takes time to get into a rhythm to last as long as she can, (and that kind of marathon is only for a fit young man), and she throws you out, shouting , 'You're not a man!', you could end up like the necrophiliac of 10 Rillington Place, who could only face doing it after he'd gassed them to death; after he'd been humiliated by the first girl he tried to have sex with who nicknamed him, 'Reggie (as in Reginald) no dick.'

....

GUILT/REGRET.

I feel guilt because I'm not getting the most out of my life, that I'm having to eke out my existence here in England without friends or a 'wife'. If, at the ripe old age of 57, I had any real cash I could, at the very least be living in a climate that suits my physical and mental makeup. No, not Bacup! I'm talking about 6,000 miles away from here where it's hot all year and there's no fear that you're going to be on your own for the rest of your natural; which is a totally unnatural concept, only acceptable here in the west.
And there's a beautiful island only a speed boat ride away where you can spend the day with your latest love interest or the regular ball and chain; a lot less painful than a rainy day in Halifax, West Yorks in late September. I feel guilt that I might not survive till I'm 65 (or 'regret' as K pointed out as an alternative word), when my lifetime of bondage and servitude should be over, and I can become an old age rover. I feel guilt because my life's not been a success, either financially or personally; I've got a bad case of , 'Oh woe is me'. Self pity hurts like hell, oh well.

....

THE DANCE OF THE SUGAR PLUM ELEPHANTS.

Imagine my delight to escape the blight of Todmorden for Halifax Town, only to be brought down by 'the dance of the sugar plum elephants'. There's a ballet school above my flat where the flat-footed twats do their training, braining any hopes I had of a speedy recovery to good mental health.
A wealth of thuds, thumps, and shock waves descend around my head on a nightly basis, causing near total stasis of my will to live. I have thought about giving the arrogant, self obsessed pest who runs this, five nights a week and all day Saturday venture, a clout or two round the head with my claw hammer,

tho' I doubt it would end like the dance macabre; I bet they'd still carry on pirouetting round her still twitching corpse as I decided who was going to get it next.

How could I have been so stupid, you might well justifiably ask, to jump straight from the frying pan into the fire? Well, dire straits call for desperate measures, and I was told at the point of signing the tenancy agreement that it wouldn't be 'that bad'; and as far as pads go, this one looked alright.

I'm now prepared to go gentle into the farthest reaches of the endless night zone, alone, listening to BBE's 'SEVEN DAYS AND ONE WEEK' eternally.

....

FOLLOWING THROUGH.

There are few worse feelings than 'following through', a spurt of liquid poo soiling your underwear. If you're lucky it will stop there and not run down your leg and on to your sock, smegma on the end of a cock couldn't smell any worse; but how would I know about that? I was never cursed with a foreskin, I've been circumcised ever since I can remember when, and I'm not that intimate with other men's cocks.

I can remember an incident over 25 years ago after a night out on the beer, waking up on the sofa in someone's shared student house about 8-o'clock in the morning. Without much warning I felt the urge 'to go', oh no! I didn't want to do a splatter job on the communal loo, so I crept out of the house like a mouse. It was right near Platt Fields Park (in Rusholme, Manchester), it wasn't dark so I thought I'd be alright; by now I really needed a shite. No one else was about; if I didn't find a toilet soon I'd have to hang my arse out over the grass.

At the very last moment I found a crapper, I think it was the parkie's own; without a moment to lose it was pants down and a full-blown dump to follow, like the one in 'DUMB AND DUMBER'. A green fug filled the air. What a bummer, there wasn't any shite paper around anywhere; I had a pair of purple underpants on that I'd never liked, so they had to do the arse-wiping job instead. I stuffed them behind the toilet bowl. My bum-hole felt lovely and fresh as I walked back out into the early summer morning, whistling a happy tune.

I could have shoved them down the pan but some poor man would have had to come along and fish them out, and spitefulness is not what I'm about. As it was, the truth would be made painfully clear when the stink from the offending purple items was brought to the inescapable attention of someone's nose; their prose would turn the air purple alright. But by that time I'd be well out of sound and sight, far, far away, on life's highway in my eternal quest to find love and romance, wearing much more sensible underpants, with a spare pair in my pocket in case the worst sort of passion killer should occur.

I had to take a 'squat' dump in a Scottish woods once, I must have wobbled a bit because some of the semi liquid stool found its way onto my pants leg; I was able to wipe myself with some lovely soft fern-like vegetation. The frustration I felt trying to rub that brown stain off my blue jeans was palpable.

Another time I was caught short, and the only place to go was in a farmer's field, I think what I left behind would help to yield a fine crop of rhubarb the following year. Gastric flu can make your poo come out as runny as consommé 'loop the loop', and enough to fill a bucket. Fuck it, I've had enough of this crap.

....

VIRGULE VIRIDITY.

It doesn't make any sense does it this title? It's not meant to really, it's just me using my pertinacity while I've still got it, and in the broadest sense of the word. After all, you can be a thrusting intellectual one year, then a few years down the line you're an incoherent wreck, like Iris Murdoch for instance; due to the onset of Alzheimer's disease. Your once so strong mind undergoes a degenerative form of dismantling, leaving you inchoate like a babbling baby.

Mental deterioration is a terrifying prospect, and I reckon that as soon as you're too far gone to remember your own name, you should be humanely put to sleep; I'd tearfully sign up for it.

Right now we're supposed to be at war against terror, though I've never seen a nation so divided against itself as ours is over Iraq. I'm a hard liner on this topic, I believe terrorists should be treated like the cowardly vermin they are, and killed like rats. As for the emotive issue of hostage taking and the inhuman and barbaric way in which they're being murdered? I haven't seen TV footage of one of them prepared to die with some dignity, they're shown whining and snivelling for their lives; they were in Iraq after all to make money, a year ago I heard that interpreters were being paid £200 a day, I wonder if they could get life insurance?

So if you're about to have your head cut off, is it best to weep quietly or hurl oaths and curses at your executioners, (they might take a bit longer to finish you off if you adopt the latter course, or scream and squeal like a stuck pig.) I might very well involuntarily opt for the last option, you just don't know do you? After all, doesn't sentient life cease once the cerebral cortex has been severed just above the spinal column? And it's got to be quicker than having your teeth pulled out with a pair of pliers, and thrown into a stinking dark cell in total agony. Or imagine another hideous scenario, you're told if you bite the head off a live rat you'll be allowed to live, so you take this squeaking and squirming thing gingerly into your hands and raise it hesitantly to your mouth; only this revolting creature's got more of an urge to live than you, and just as you open your mouth it lunges forward and bites your tongue and won't let go, and starts to shit and piss all over your hands, total nightmare or what!?

I hate the false sentimentality that's going on in our country right now, the way we're backtracking we deserve to be overrun by Al Qaeda and its totalitarian, blood-soaked doctrine of total terror. Of course I'll be condemned for exercising my right to freedom of speech, (not that anyone's going to read this in a hurry), and unlike our prime minister who, if he's hounded out of office, can look forward to a luxuriously comfortable retirement, (I think his missus has just bought a house for £3.6 million; now that's what I call making the law work for you), I can look forward to more social isolation than I already endure.

Well, I can live with that, I'm already out of synch' with modern British society, and at times I wish I had the courage to go and lay my neck on a cold railway line, and wait for the train to come without flinching away at the very last moment. If I wasn't in acute physical decline I wouldn't think this way, and that's a fact.

The collective title for the 306 page, typed-up manuscript (my last 'big job') that I want to put on disc is: 'IF GOD IS HOPE, AND HOPE SPRINGS ETERTNAL, HOW COME THERE'S SO LITTLE OF IT REFLECTED IN MY WORK?' Health-wise I live from day to day now, I don't know how long I've got before I'm too riddled with arthritis to carry on working at what's turned out to be a lost cause for me. Hope does spring eternal; it's the driving force that keeps us going from day to day, those of us who decidedly don't lead charmed lives anyway. At least, short of suicide, we won't give up and keep our ugly mugs out of happy healthy people's faces. We'll keep on depressing them for as long as we can…and then some.

(Some tentative good fortune has come my way since I originally penned the above, also I've discovered the curative powers of Glocosamine Sulphate, it's proved to be very beneficial for me, if only I'd found out about it earlier. It can stimulate the mind as well as the body.) (That fad didn't last long.)

....

YOU ARE WHAT YOU EXCRETE. (Could this be a toilet humour 'bloomer'?)

I hate old people, they shuffle round like pigeons, taking up valuable space, pecking away at what's left of their lives, too shit-scared to die, eking it out from day to day; I hope it's 5,000 old people who're dying every year from MRSA, (apart from that mediocre actress with the 'trout pout' who led Tony out of MEN BEHAVING BADLY to involuntarily lose control of some vital body fluid while they were in a sack race together, because she'd prick teased him for so long, and it was his only chance to be up against her; she didn't die, she just suffered sadly as part of a general slide in her fortunes.)
With more and more of us 'wrinklies' coming on tap each year, falling into the poverty trap; but more than willing to hang in there as long as we can, after all isn't 60 the new 40? And the three-score-years-and-ten span the new clapped-out 50? Nifty old fuckers sucking the life blood out of the world, full of bitterness and contempt; I'd rather be exempt from all that, at least here in the UK. I'll go and play at being 'forever young' (didn't the 65-year-old Bob Dylan write a song of the same title back in the 1960s when he was still highly credible? Unlike now, the boring old fart) in Thailand. (And don't go jumping to the wrong conclusions, I'm not a kiddy fiddler, anyone over 16 [female] is fair game in my book, biologically speaking.)

....

ANOTHER DAY IN THE DARK.

This clapped-out model comes complete with built in fatigue and depression, a wannabe knickers sniffer and gusset licker. He could only get access to used 'panties' or thongs through specialist websites, and he'd prefer to abuse these items while they were still warm, freshly taken off by the wearer. But he'd never had a real girlfriend, when he was young and highly sensitive, it had been made painfully clear to him that he wasn't attractive to the opposite sex, even though he was born to spend his life worshipping them.
He was gripped by a reassuring sense of hopelessness, as he lay curled up in the dark with only the radio for company, on low in the background. He wished the night would last forever so he'd never have to get up or face the world again; the nauseous pain in his guts was a manifestation of self-pity, another form of debility. Too much harsh and negative reality had ruined his health, now even if fame and wealth came his way, he feared it would be too late to enjoy celebrity. Girls might throw their oestrogen-scented panties at

him during performances from his deathbed, but he'd be too far gone to masturbate furiously with a still warm pair of them over his nose.

....

POETRY, UNMASKED AND EXPOSED.

The formulae of traditional, or conventional poetry, sucks to me; its highbrow obscurity appealing only to the scholarly few. I've read and listened to enough of the stuff to know that not only do I not get it, (it makes me feel less intelligent than I know I am), but that I FUCKING HATE IT!!! Most of it's depressing bilge, reeking of mothballs and polite decay.
It's about time poetry was unmasked and the question asked, how come these colossal bores, dinosaur-like in their intransigence, have still got such a restrictive hold on a metre that should be fun? Along the lines of, 'There was a young man from Ealing who reckoned he could hit the ceiling with his spunk when he came. He wanked himself off, gave a loud cough and said in a few minutes he'd try again, because this time his love slime had only gone as far as the end of his nose, and it looked like a dewdrop; his girlfriend mopping it off with her keks. He should have had sex with her between her tits, (a tit fuck), then she would have had to move her head quick before she got an eyeful. Show me the man who can stick his erect member into a bowl of trifle and keep it, and I'll show you how to steep it in larks tongues and aspic, with a cherry on the tip.'

....

THE WORLD ORDER ACCORDING TO OSAMAR BIN LADEN AND THE TALIBAN.

No man, woman or child would be safe from the random wrath of these totalitarian monsters, they would make the nazi excesses look like child's play; these people are wholly evil.

!!
!!

AXIOMATIC APOPHTHEGMS AND APHORISTIC ADAGES. ('What's that spell, what's that spell'? MAXIM by four other ways on the road to hell.)

I shamelessly begged for a few crumbs from an obscenely rich man's table, but he felt he wasn't able to throw me any; he didn't even offer to sell me a few or tell me to get in the queue. So I thought, 'Fuck you Felix Dennis', I'll write this about you. Old hippies don't die or fade away, they go and play at being the great virid philanthropist to while their idle hours away. And let's face it, when your many millions have been made out of ink and paper, it's as well to protect your breeding stock, around the clock if necessary. (It rhymes Felix, it rhymes.)

....

WORDISM.

I fell foul of a manipulative 'politically correct' poetry teacher last night, if she'd have been a bloke it could have run to a fight, though I would have played my, 'I'm nearly blind' card to wriggle out of it. She's an anti racist, homosexual-loving zealot, as hot as mustard on these tiresome issues; I hope she needs tissues to dry her eyes after my surprise attack, implying that women are at their best when they're on their backs, with erect penises in their clacks…lip-smackingly gorgeous! (I also pointed out that as a native born Briton with disabilities, I've been discriminated against all my life; this cut no ice with her.)

....

The next two pieces I sent to Felix Dennis, publisher and poet, currently estimated to be the 65th richest man in the UK, worth around £585 million; and the man who's so pretentious he had to go and find himself a publisher for his highbrow, longwinded poetry, (you should see the company poem he penned for Dennis Publishing, mindbendingly boring). Random House was probably so afraid that if they turned him down, he'd take them over, they decided to publish him instead. And do you know, there are thousands of silly fuckers out there who've bought his crap! The only thing I can say in his defence is, he publishes VIZ so he can't be all-bad.

This next piece, the third to the last in this, my last collection, was inspired by a website I stumbled across called: www.circleofpoets.com, an American project. I typed a copy of my 'PLACE YOUR FAITH IN YOURSELF' poem on its web page, with a view to winning $5000, as advertised. It turned out to be a 'vanity publishing' scam; I couldn't send them e-mails because their site was blocked. So I wrote this next piece on their web page, which wasn't very flattering about them, and I received an e-mail back a few days later saying I'd been selected again to go in their expensive anthology; are they 'mad for it' or what?

IS THERE ANYBODY OUT THERE?

I've tried e-mailing you twice, but messages cannot be sent, my server can't make a connection; the only message I'm getting from you is, 'Send $49 pdq (pretty damn quick!). Thankfully, I'm not thick enough to do that, I don't know if you have the word 'twat' in the US of A, but hey! I'm not a silly one. My creative juices have all dried up, my cup runneth over with bile; there're so many people who'll smile to your face but who're only interested in screwing you for every penny they can. Hey man, we've all got to make a living, but there are no prizes for giving and not receiving, even a hard-bound, coffee table book of verse; well I suppose at its worse it could make a good draught excluder. I'd be ruder if social etiquette allowed, along the lines of, 'You can shove it up your arse sideways on!'
I'd love to be big in America like Bukowski, the existentialist writer of invective and every day strain; I've been at it long enough; it's as unrelentingly tough at the bottom as it is at the top of the heap. I go to sleep dreaming of being a success, and wake up to the same old mess my life's always been…a bad dream in a bad reality. C'mon, take pity on me and find me a genuine deal, a huge advance on a body of work already signed and sealed, it just needs to be delivered, stick a fork in me and turn me over, I'm done.

....

THE IRRATIONAL IRRITABILITY OF THE INVOLUNTARILY ECONOMICALLY INACTIVE?

The Lotto fund for good causes is a nest egg for the rich and well-to-do to tap into when they don't want to spend any of their own cash; it's mainly poor trash like me who hand over their benefit money in the faint hope of winning enough to free them from this yoke of state-owned slavery. If I had a stately pile or an opera company, they'd be bending over backwards to sponsor me, but as it is they'd wilfully ignore me if I asked for a mill' or two to improve my own circumstances; I'd stand more chances if I set up a 'Dances With Wolves' ballet company, using classically trained wolves of course.

Some days my head is nearly exploding with an enthusiastic lust for life, but there's no realistic outlet to channel this creative energy into; I have lucrative ideas but they plummet like lead balloons into a hot lake of liquid sulphur, the resultant stench is appalling.

At other times my involuntary economical inactivity leaves me feeling so frustrated, I feel actively anti social; a more determined member of the underclass would go out to rob and steal to redress this anomalous imbalance, not being unduly concerned whether they used violence to get what they wanted. Me? I'm too afraid of a prison environment to risk involuntary incarceration. So I stay at home seething with impotent rage, stabbing the page with my pen, again and again and again, until I feel relief flooding into my veins and I can fall into a satisfied sleep.

It takes guts to throw yourself in front of a moving train, I know I could never do it; it also takes guts to live on or near the poverty line and decide to soldier on through it, no matter how much it pains you to feel your life wasting away in a society obsessed with gain. I've just put some music on to soothe my aching chest, it's doing me some good, much more than Prozac ever could. Now if I can win Saturday night's lotto jackpot my money worries will be at an end, hope is a very consoling friend. (Needless to say, I was only 6 numbers away from winning.)

....

COUGH OFF.
(Anyone concerned only with matters of good taste should stop here, but if you've got this far you can't be that particular can you? 14/11/04.)

I hate being around anyone who openly coughs, it's a virus's way of spreading its infection to other people; last year I caught a near fatal dose of flu (after having a flu jab) off some arsehole coughing his guts up on a long bus journey I was on; his germs made a beeline straight for me. I reckoned that if I'd still been a smoker this flu attack would have finished me off, as it was, it was one of the worst weeks of my life, respirationally speaking.

Three nights ago I suffered a severe bout of acid reflux, it woke me up in the middle of the night with burning indigestion and a feverish feeling; earlier that day I'd begun to have a chesty cough which I related to catching off someone who works in the Access room at Halifax central library; a perfectly pleasant lady who'd recently had a bad cold and cough. When she coughed she just let rip, making no attempt to cover her mouth, I tried tutting, and muttering loudly under my breath, and groaning, but it had no effect. Eventually, after what seemed like an age of internal torment, I was violently sick...four times! Relief at last, I went back to bed shivering and moaning. I had some important (yes me) things to do at the library the next morning that couldn't be put off, so feeling slightly better I braved the cold drizzle to get there early, to be greeted by coughing Susan. I gritted my teeth and got on with it. Two hours later I was back home, and not long after, the previous night's symptoms returned despite the fact I'd hardly eaten or drank anything since the previous evening; I resigned myself to the grim prospect of going back to bed to ride the fever out.

Not long after I'd crawled in between the sheets, I had to dart out again to be sick twice, closely followed by an evil smelling bowel evacuation of liquid manure; what a sorry plight I was in. Thankfully I knew that on this particular day, there would be little or no noise polluting torment from the dance school above my flat, so I could be ill in peace, with Radio 4 on low in the background to keep me company as I came in and out of consciousness. At some point in the afternoon I experienced what I thought were a series of 'wet farts', the type that make you think you might have had a nasty accident but haven't, so I feverishly dozed off again. Imagine my horror when sometime later, my worst fears had been realised, some faecal matter had escaped my sphincter control; another dash to the toilet to clean myself up, still feeling as rough as fuck, to use the vernacular.

The last time I had this kind of gastric accident was in a flat I was renting in Walsden; the bedroom was ice-cold and I couldn't afford to keep the ineffective central heating on for very long at a time. Not long after I moved in I developed this gastric flu, and had some involuntary leakage onto my rented mattress, OH NO! And on that occasion the unwelcome rectal mucus smelt! Not horribly, but enough to cause me to rub the stain frantically and repeatedly with after shave, and turn the mattress over; I washed the sheets in my new washing machine...eventually. Imagine the situation, you're feeling near death's door when this sort of anti social thing happens. At its worse it could cause you to have to throw your soiled mattress and bedding out, which reminds me, (one final aside, I promise) some years ago I saw this homosexual on TV who was dying of AIDS, the most memorable thing he said was, bitterly, 'All same sex is, is a pain in the arse and a shit-stained duvet'; let that be a warning to all you indeterminate young men out there who're thinking of venturing into bottom exploring.

Now, if you can remember that far back, I'd just wiped myself clean using kitchen towel, it being more absorbent than mere toilet paper. All I wanted to do was get back into bed so I could start burning up again and die politely. But when I got back there, there it was, a tell tale stain on the bottom sheet, oh fuck! But I'd noticed the watery liquid I'd wiped off the backs of my upper thighs hadn't smelt, so gingerly I put my nose to this dark smear, NO

ODOUR! I rubbed at it with my discarded underpants, still no reek, so I discarded them again. When I got in it felt cold and wet, an unsavoury 'wet patch', but my body was so hot with the ague it soon dried up; I reckon I was really lucky there, and that sheet will last another week before I need to change it, (only joking.)
I reckon they should ban people from openly coughing in public, as well as smoking; they're both life threatening diseases. I now regard writing as a disease, and I wish I'd never been bitten by the bug; it's only made a mug out of me; will you ever read this honey and still have some time for me? (To k.) (I've had some hot wanks on her memory I can tell you; it serves her right for going out of my life completely with hardly a backward glance. Cheers K.)

....